MATHEMATICS
A MASTER FILE
KEY STAGE 1

Compiled by
D C Perkins, BA (Hons), MEd, PhD (Wales) and E J Perkins, BSc (Hons), MEd
Illustrations by Anthony James

These Master Files are designed for use in the classroom. Each consists of teachers' notes, pupils' resource material, worksheets, activities and record sheet. Each book covers a part of the national curriculum in depth allowing the teacher to decide the amount of material to use according to the age and ability of the children.

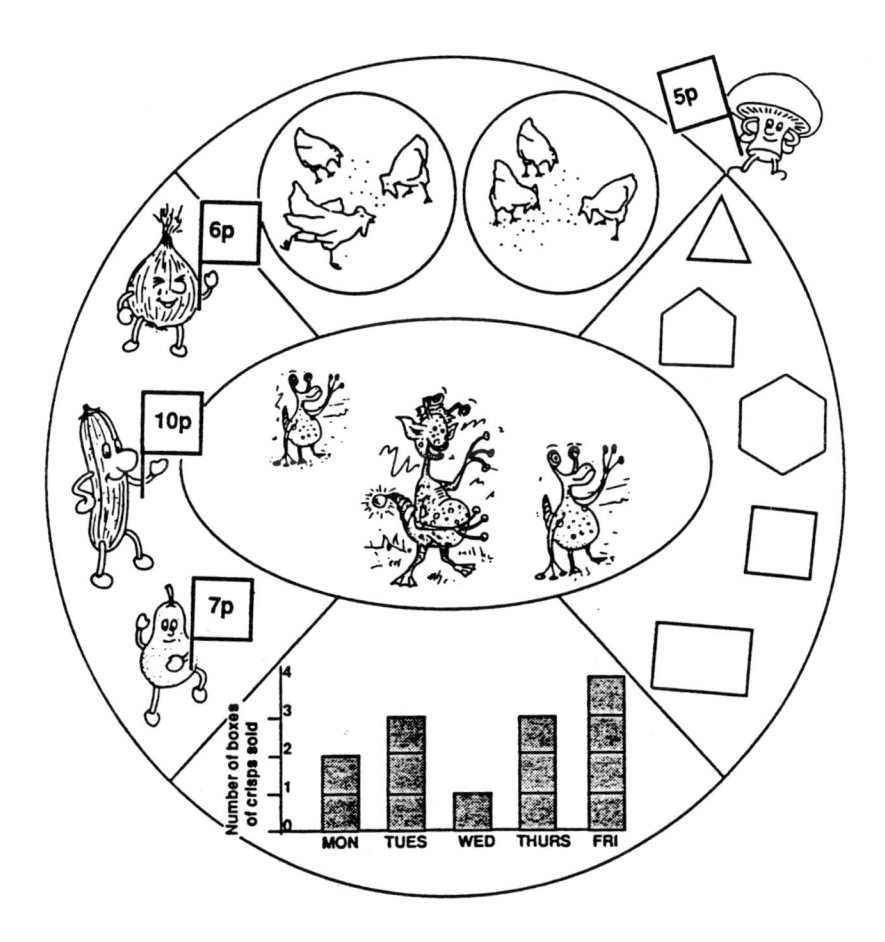

All rights reserved. This book is not copyright free. It is sold subject to the condition that it shall not, by way of trade or otherwise, be lent, hired out or otherwise circulated without the publisher's written consent. No part of this publication may be reproduced, stored in a retrieval system, or transmitted, in any form or by any means, electronic, mechanical, photocopying, recording or otherwise without the prior written permission of the publisher. All pages in this book can be photocopied for educational purposes only within the purchasing school or educational establishment. There is no limit to the number of copies that may be produced within the purchasing school or establishment and no return in respect of any photocopying licence is needed. This permission does not extend to the making of copies (e.g. in a resource centre) for use outside the institution in which they are made, nor to the making of copies for hire or re-sale.

DOMINO BOOKS (WALES) LTD
SWANSEA SA1 1FN
Tel. 01792 459378   Fax. 01792 466337
Maths Master File KS1 © EJP & DCP 1995
Reprinted 1995, 1996, 1997
ISBN 1 85772 107 1

CONTENTS 1

PUPILS' RESOURCES/WORKSHEETS

	Page		Page
NUMBER		An Add 3 Robot	48
Colour to Sort	4	A Take Away 4 Robot	49
Sorting as Sets	5	Multiplication and Counting On	50
Sorting by Type	6	2, 5, and 10 (Hundred Square)	51
Match and Colour	7	Multiply Squares	52
Matching Shapes	8	Bingo (Multiplication)	53
How Many?	9	Tens and Units	54
Counting Objects	10	Matching Numbers	55
Writing and Counting Numbers (1, 2)	11	Bingo (Addition)	56
Writing and Counting Numbers (3, 4)	12	Sums to 20	57
Writing and Counting Numbers (5, 6, 7)	13	Sums to 20	58
Counting	14	Numbers to 1000	59
Writing and Counting Numbers (8, 9)	15	Numbers to 1000	60
Counting to 10	16	Numbers in Words	61
Add 1	17	Division	62
1 to 10	18	Multiplication	63
Snow White (1 - 10)	19	Units	64
Flowers (3, 4, 5)	20	Measuring	65
Conservation of Numbers	21	Money	66
Addition	22	Time	67
Add	23	More Time	68
Make 5	24	Negative Numbers	69
Make 10	25	Lists	70
How Many Leaves?	26	Linking	71
Take Away Strips	27	Count and Record	72
Subtraction	28	Picture Graphs	73
Add or Subtract	29	Picture Graphs	74
Add (Vertical Addition)	30	Waiting for the Bus	75
Take Away (Vertical Subtraction)	31	Bar Graphs	76
Find the Missing Numbers	32	Weather Chart	77
Estimates	33	Sorting and Recording	78
Left Luggage	34		
Ordering	35	**SHAPE AND SPACE**	
Catch a Falling Star	36	Position	79
Money	37	Measuring Words	80
Shopping	38	2-D Shapes	81
Car Boot Sale	39	3-D Shapes	82
Half	40	Matching Shapes and Sides	83
Quarter	41	Angles	84
Measuring using Non-Standard Units	42	Moving	85
Measuring and Comparing	43	Symmetry	86
Measures - Standard Units	44	Co-ordinates	87
Patterns - Shapes and Colours	45	Points of the Compass	88
Number Bonds	46	Clockwise or Anti-clockwise?	89
Odd and Even Numbers	47		

Teachers' Notes and Resources Contents on next page.

CONTENTS 2

TEACHERS' NOTES AND RESOURCES

	Page		*Page*
HOW TO USE YOUR MASTER FILE	iii	Calculators	94
		Investigations and Problem Solving	94
TEACHERS' NOTES AND RESOURCES	90	Data	94
		Lists and Tables	95
NUMBER		Graphs and Data	95
Using Maths	91	Venn Digrams	95
Early Counting	91	Carroll Diagrams	95
Addition	91	Co-Ordinates	95
Subtraction	91		
Estimating	91	**SHAPE AND SPACE**	
Ordering	91	2-D Shapes	96
Money	92	Angles	96
Halves and Quarters	92	3-D Shapes	96
Measuring and Units	92	Words of position	96
Numbers in Words and Figures	92	Movement	96
Sums to 10 and 20	92	Symmetry	96
Numbers to 1000	92		
Multiplication and Division	92	**MISCELLANEOUS**	
Number Patterns	92	Hundred Square	97
Relationships Between Different Operations	93	Attribute Cards	98
Function Machines	93	Two-Centimetre Squared Paper	99
Time	93	Centimetre Squared Paper	100
Zero and Negative Numbers	93	Dotty Paper (Squares)	101
Sorting	94	Dotty Paper (Triangles)	102
'Weight'	94	Record Sheet	103

HOW TO USE YOUR MASTER FILE

For many experienced teachers these few lines will seem superfluous. This book follows the guidelines of the National Curriculum Order for Mathematics. The maths learned depends on the child's ability. By the end of Key Stage 1, most pupils should be able to cope with the material in Levels 1 to 3. By the end of Key Stage 2, they should be able to cope with the material in Levels 2 - 5. The contents of each level is laid out in the National Curriculum. Some of the worksheets are more difficult than others. There is plenty of material that all will find interesting and fun to tackle and other work that is more challenging. We do not envisage any problems selecting appropriate material.

The scope of the material taught in mathematics today has widened considerably and the emphasis on relating the subject to 'real' situations in the 'real' world makes the subject less mysterious and of more obvious use. A sound understanding of the fundamental theory is essential but so is an awareness that tedious repetition creates nothing but boredom. It is when children are little, when everything is new that the foundations of mathematical ability are developed, interest generated or lost.

1. All the material in this book is photocopiable as defined on the first page. This means that all the material can be used in any way you wish in the classroom situation. Drawings can be photocopied and adapted for further work.

2. Covering sections of the master copies with plain paper enables resource material to be used in different ways.

3. Reduction of the A4 master copies to A5 means that they can be pasted in children's exercise books. The master copies can also be enlarged to A3 making it easier for students to work on them as a group.

4. Some of the photocopies can be cut to make additional puzzles and games.

5. It is intended that the material should be used selectively depending on the ages and abilities of your pupils.

6. Much of the completed work may be used as visual aids around the classroom.

7. Remember, there are often several ways in which problems can be tackled.

8. Project work may be done individually, in groups and/or with teacher participation.

9. Mathematics is important in most subjects and these links underpin some of the reasons for learning the subject. There is latitude and longitude and navigation in geography, dating discoveries in history and archaeology and making computer pictures of what they were like . . . Concepts learned now are essential later in engineering, architecture, economics, all the sciences . . . Where practical, links with other subjects should be used.

10. Mathematics is about pattern, sorting, classifying and organising. Much of the work in this book can be used to illustrate the importance of these skills in the 'real' world.

We hope you enjoy using this book and welcome any comments.

Colour to sort

Colour the apples red, the bananas yellow and the pears green.

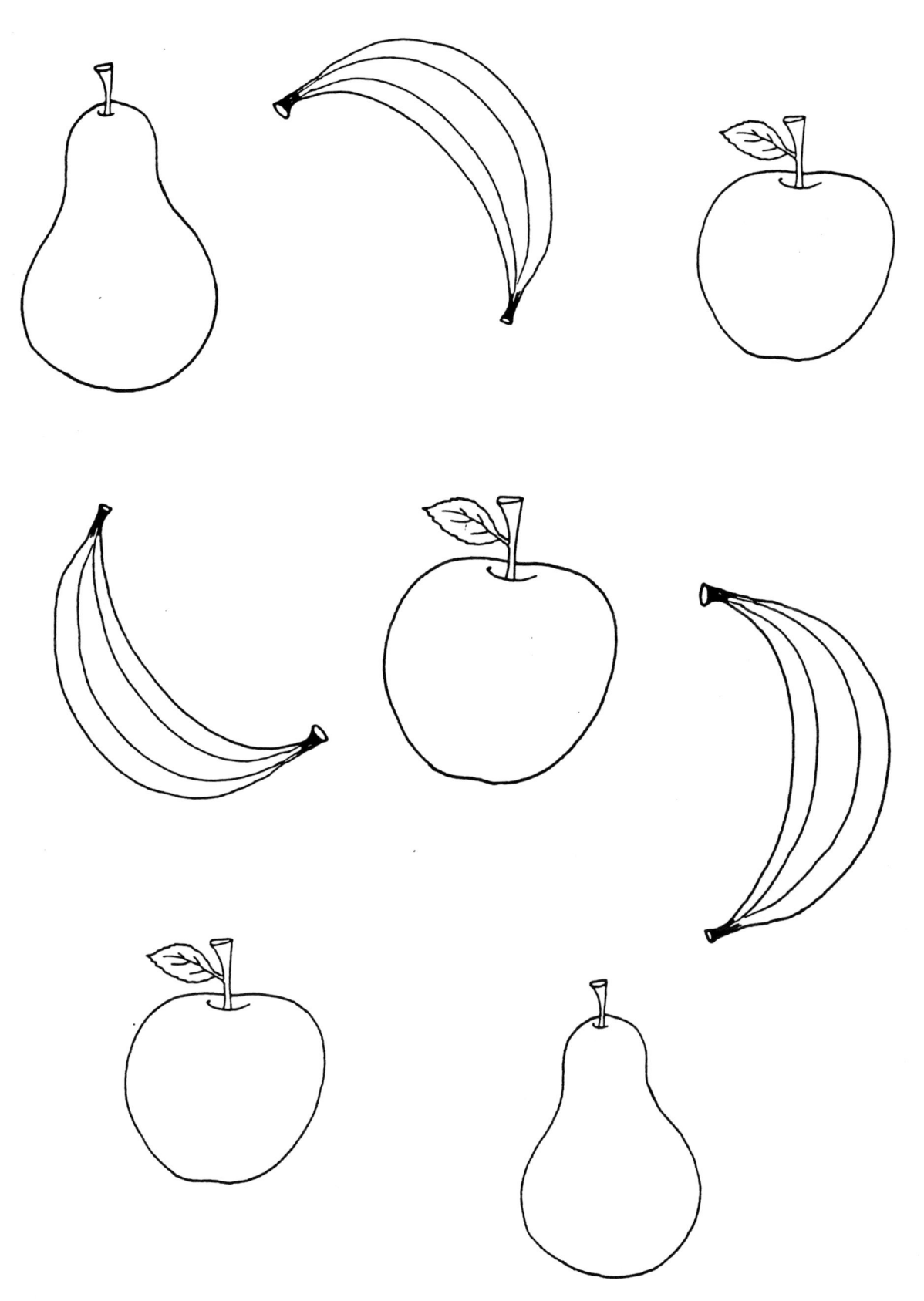

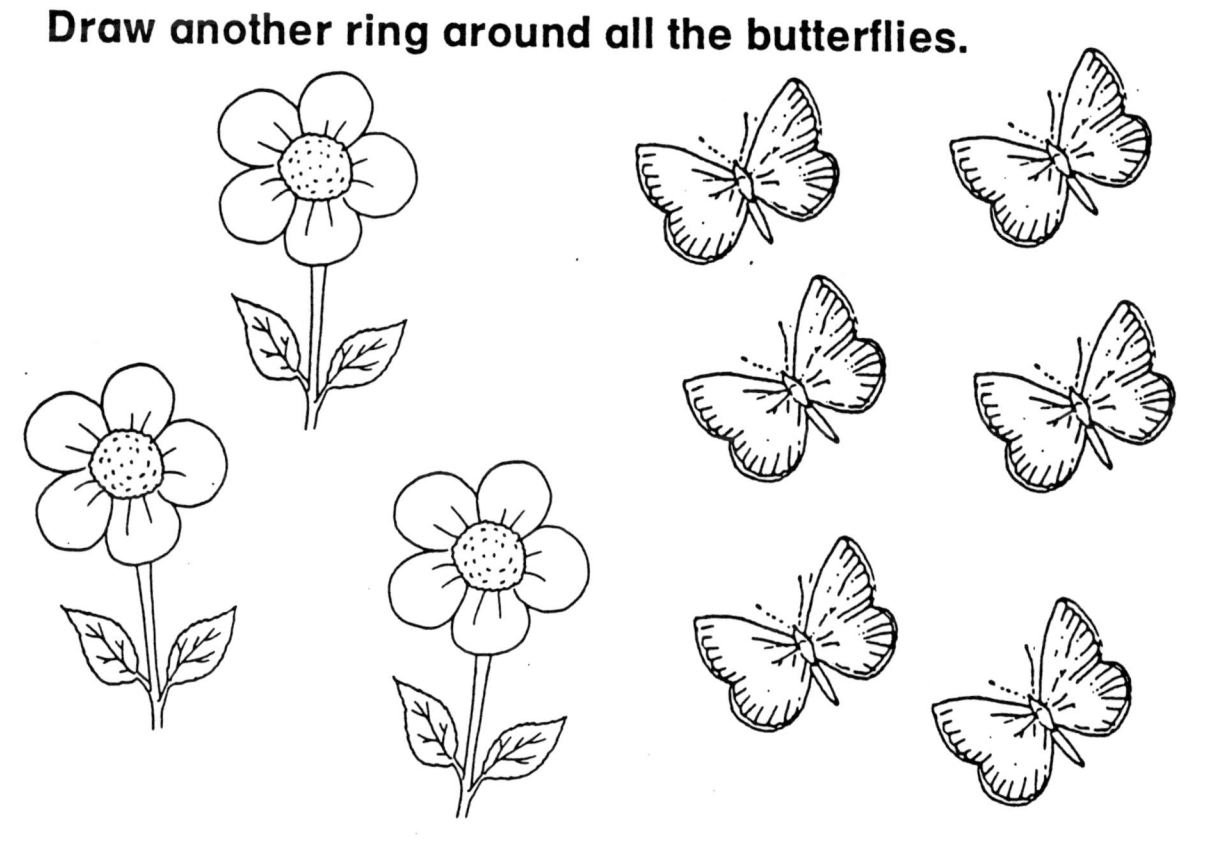

Sorting

Fill this ring with balloons and colour them red.

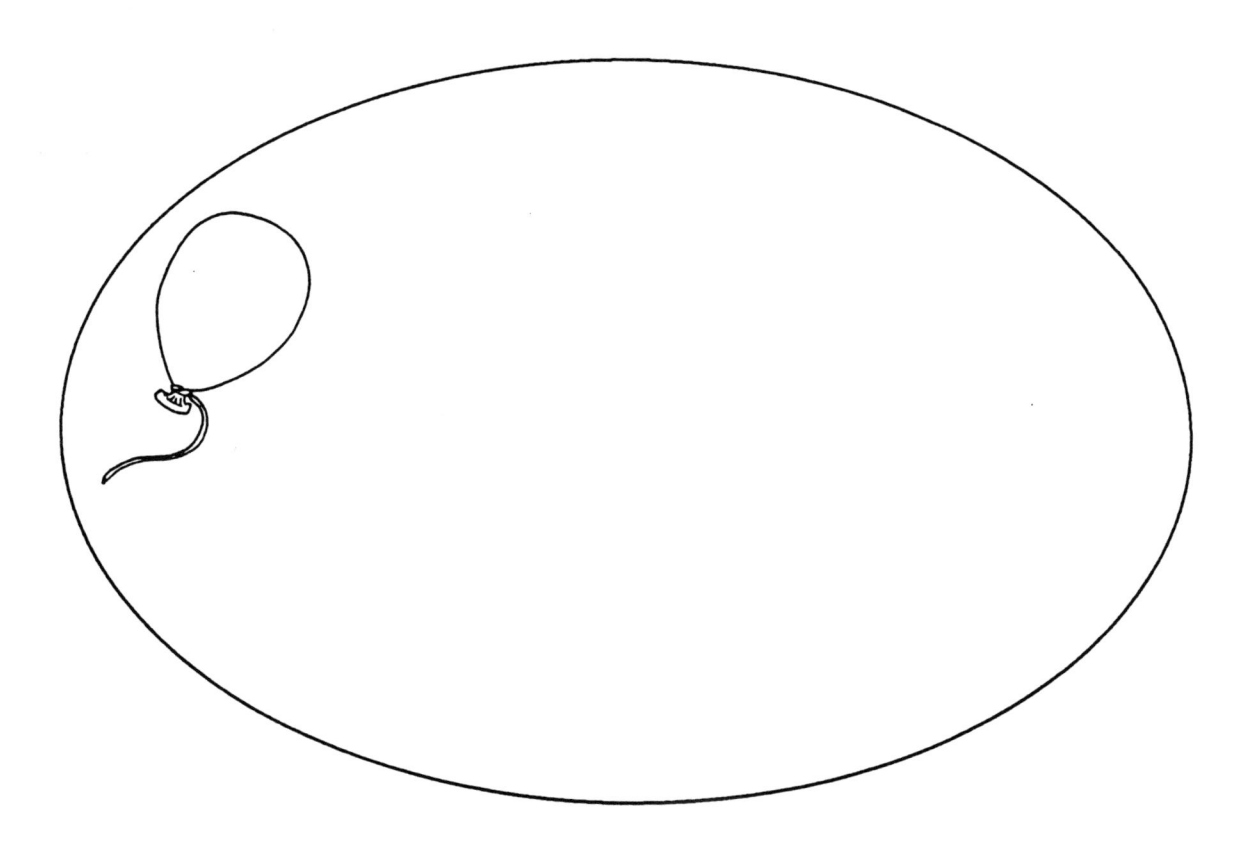

Colour the flowers and the butterflies.
Draw a ring around all the flowers.
Draw another ring around all the butterflies.

Sorting

Here are two families of dogs. Colour the picture and then draw a ring around one family.

Colour the picture and then draw a ring around all the puppies.

What are outside the ring, big dogs or puppies?

Match and colour

Draw lines to join the things which are the same then colour the pictures.

Which of these things do you wear in school?

Two things which go together like two gloves are called pairs. How many pairs can you find?

Matching shapes

Draw lines to match this family and their shadows.

Maths KS1 Master File © EJP and DCP

Number Level 1 Matching Shapes 8

How many?

Draw lines to show how many animals are in each set.

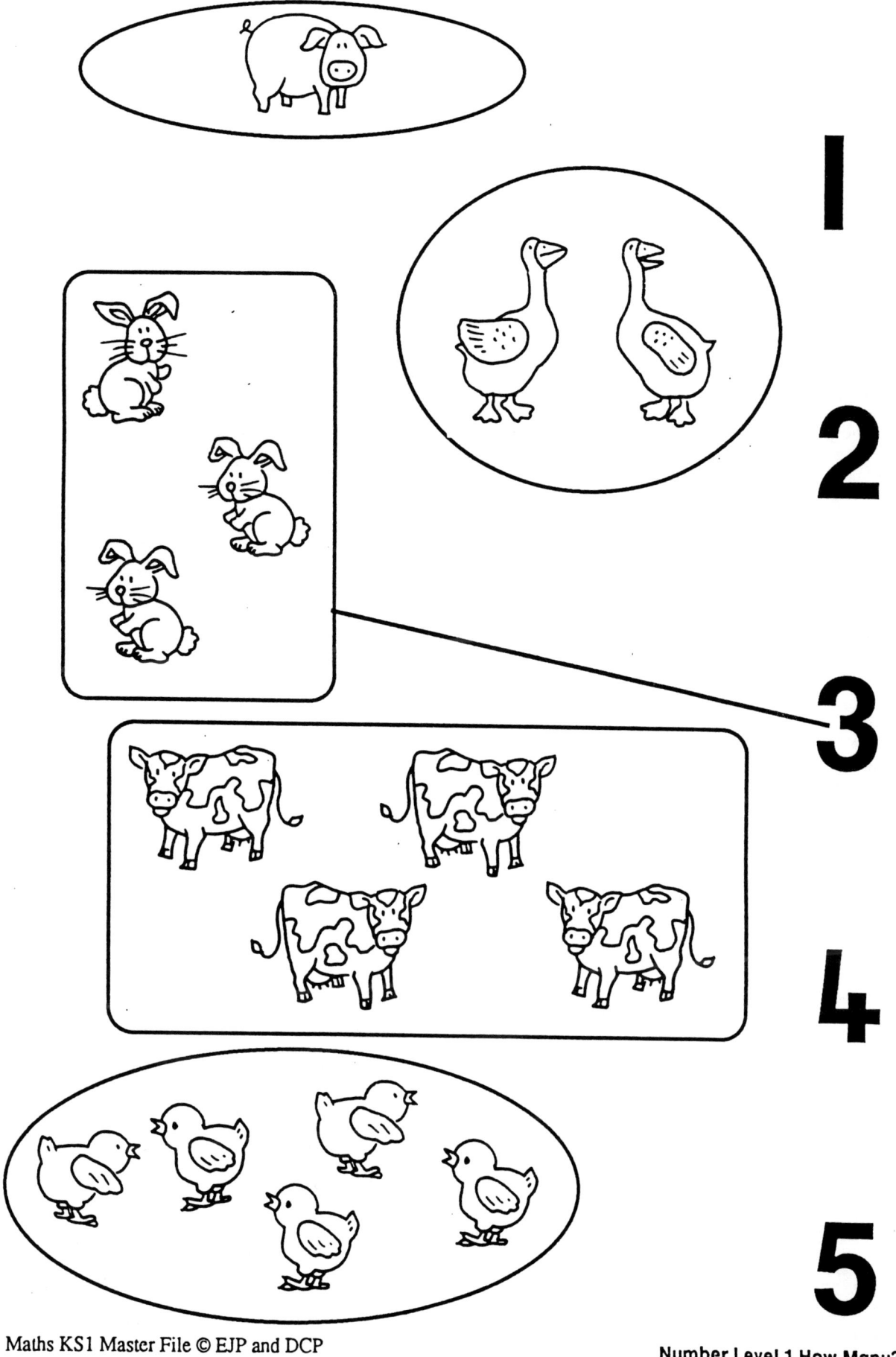

1

2

3

4

5

Maths KS1 Master File © EJP and DCP

Counting objects

Join each mouse to a piece of cheese.

Join each bucket to a spade.
How many spades are left over?

Join each lolly to a stick.
How many sticks are missing?

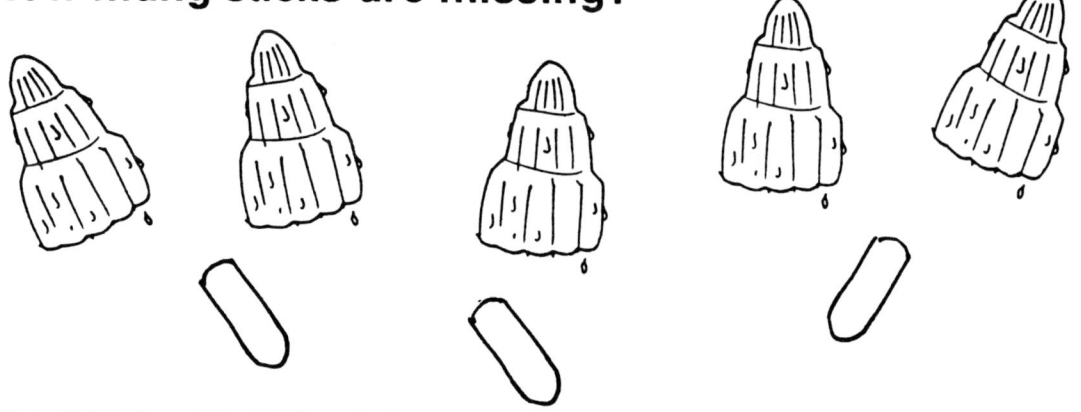

Write numbers

Write **1** ┆ ┆ ┆ ┆ ┆ ┆

Write **2** 2 2 2 2 2 2

Write 1 or 2 in the boxes.

☐ hen

☐ horses

☐ pig

☐ cows

☐ rabbits

☐ ducks

Write numbers

Write **3** 3 3 3 3 3 3

Write **4** 4 4 4 4 4 4

Write 1, 2, 3 or 4 in the boxes.

sheep ☐

chicks ☐

frogs ☐

puppies ☐

rabbits ☐

ladybirds ☐

crocodile ☐

snakes ☐

Writing numbers

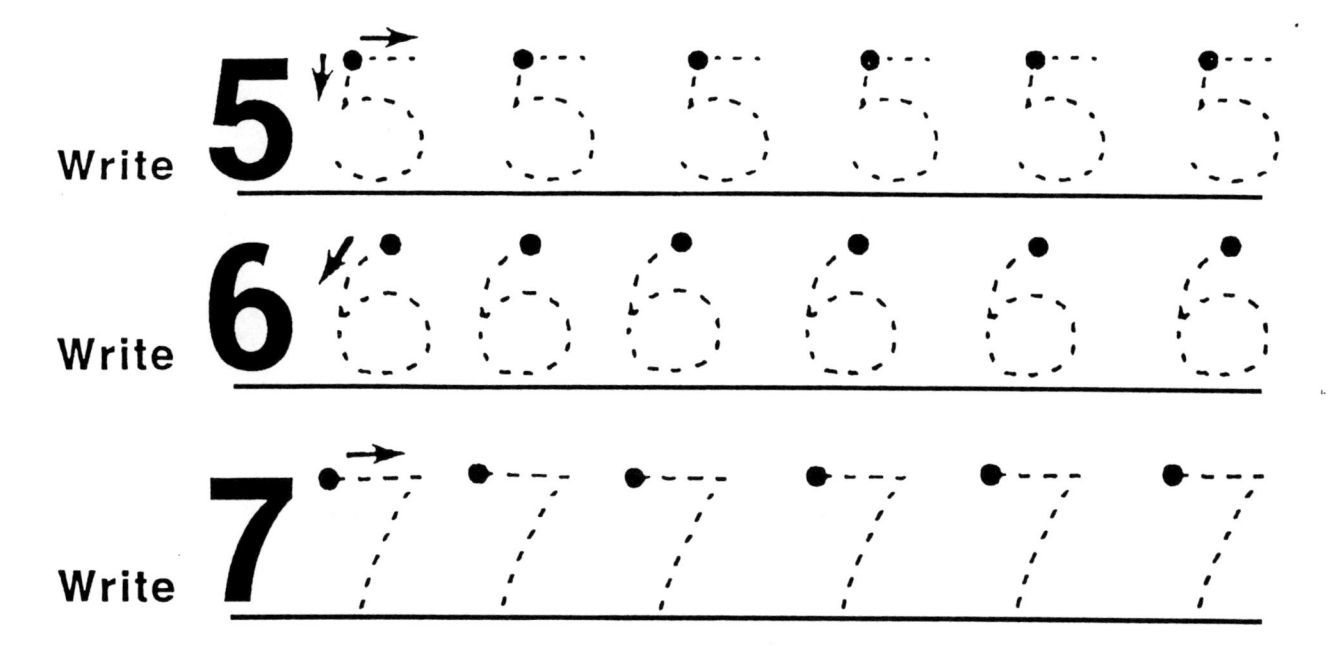

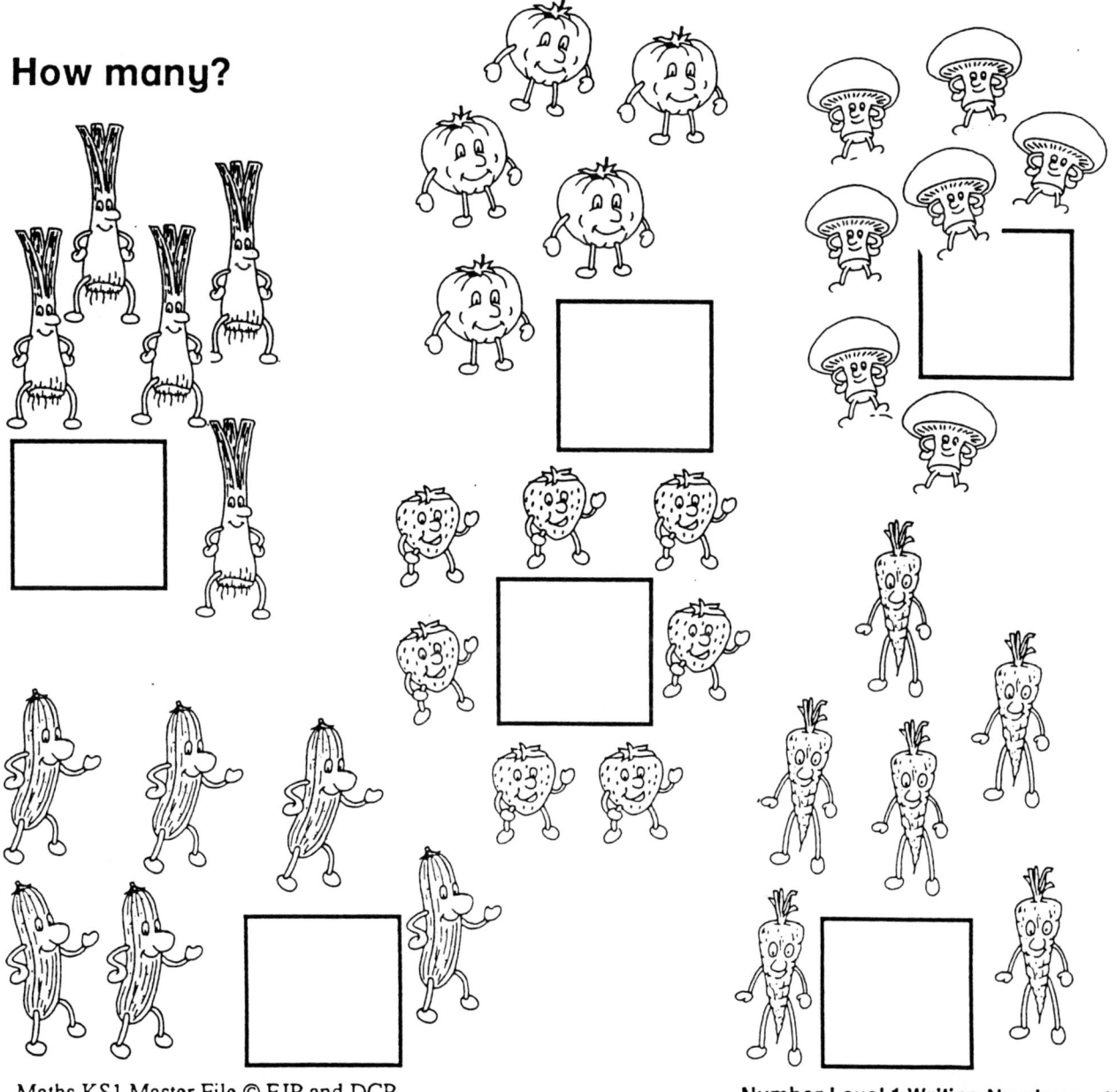

Write **5** 5 5 5 5 5 5 5

Write **6** 6 6 6 6 6 6 6

Write **7** 7 7 7 7 7 7 7

How many?

Counting

Draw 5 spots on the ladybird.

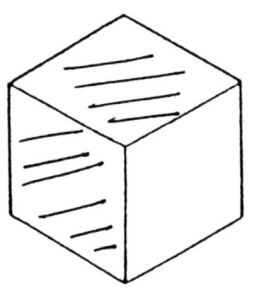

Draw 6 dots on the die.

Draw 4 buttons on the clown's shirt.

Draw 3 petals on the flower.

Draw 2 windows and 1 door on the house.

Draw 3 stars in the sky

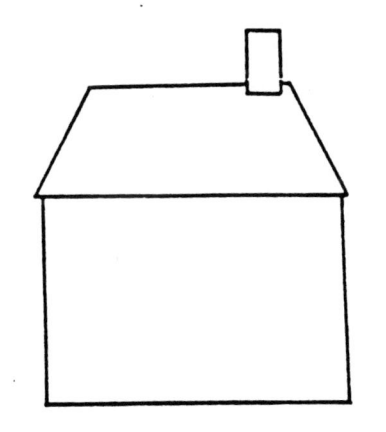

Write numbers

Write **8** 8 8 8 8 8 8

Write **9** 9 9 9 9 9 9

How many arms? ☐

How many tentacles? ☐

How many leaves? ☐

How many bones?
(Don't forget the
one in his mouth.) ☐

How many whiskers? ☐

How many legs? ☐

Counting to 10

Count and colour the egg cups. Draw different patterns on them.

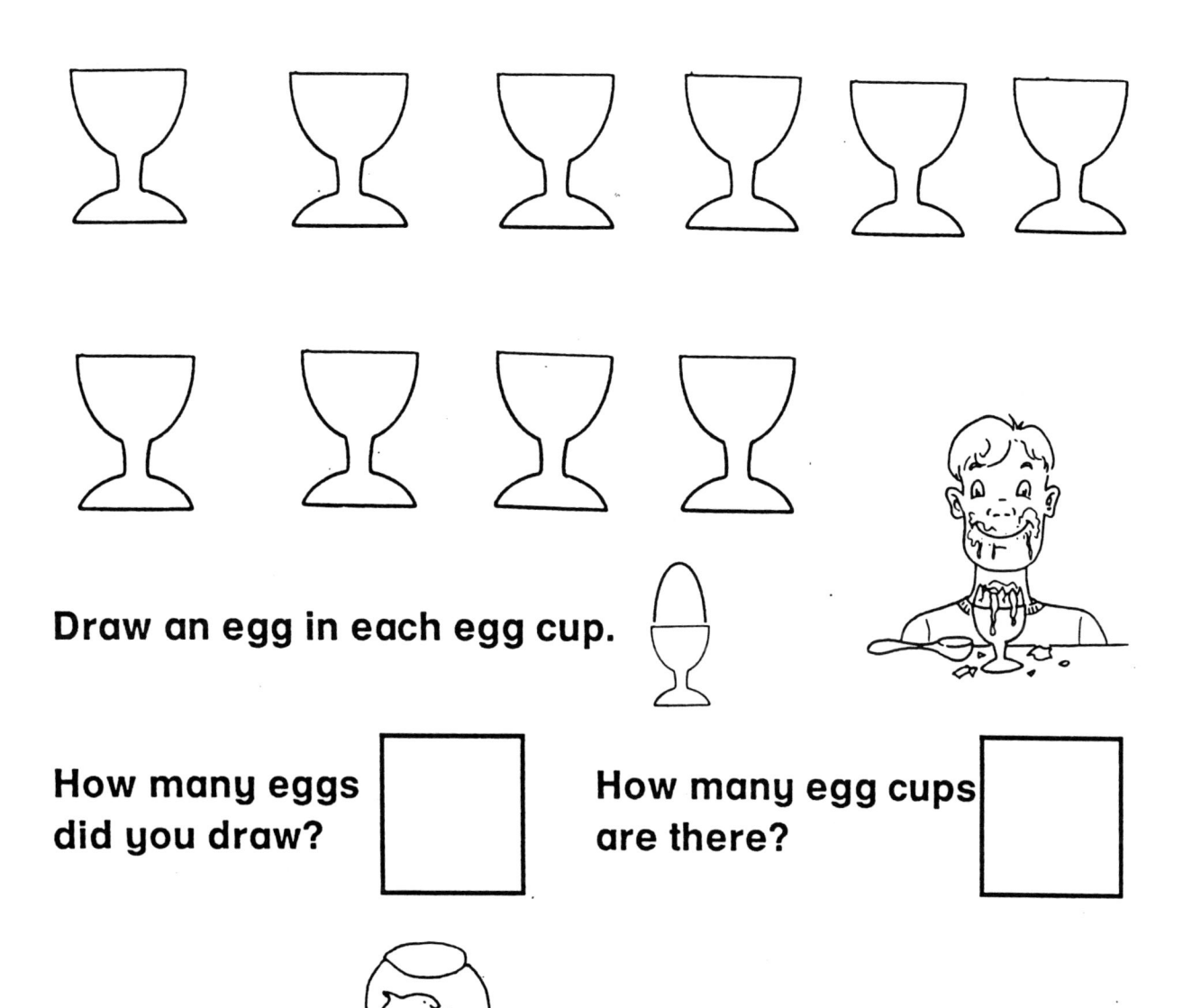

Draw an egg in each egg cup.

How many eggs did you draw?

How many egg cups are there?

Draw 6 bowls.
Draw a fish in each bowl.

How many fish did you draw?

Add 1

Draw 1 more. How many now?

strawberries

lemons

apples

pears

bananas

oranges

1 to 10

Join the dots and colour the pictures.

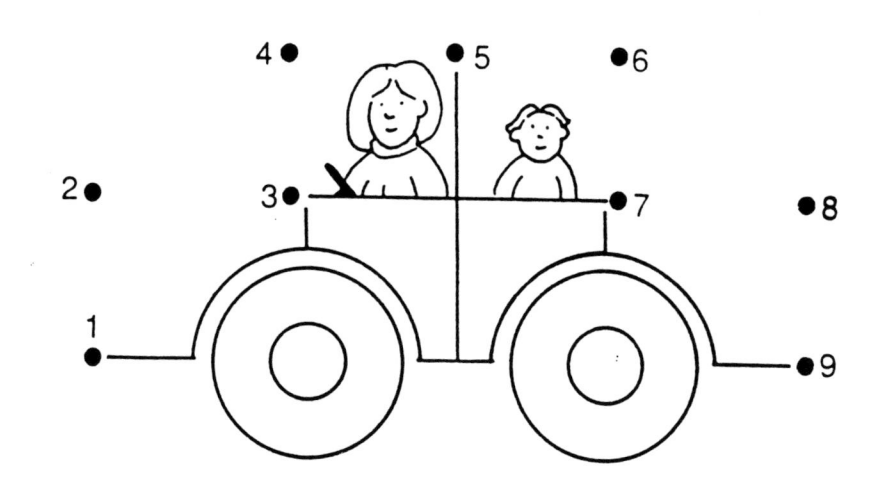

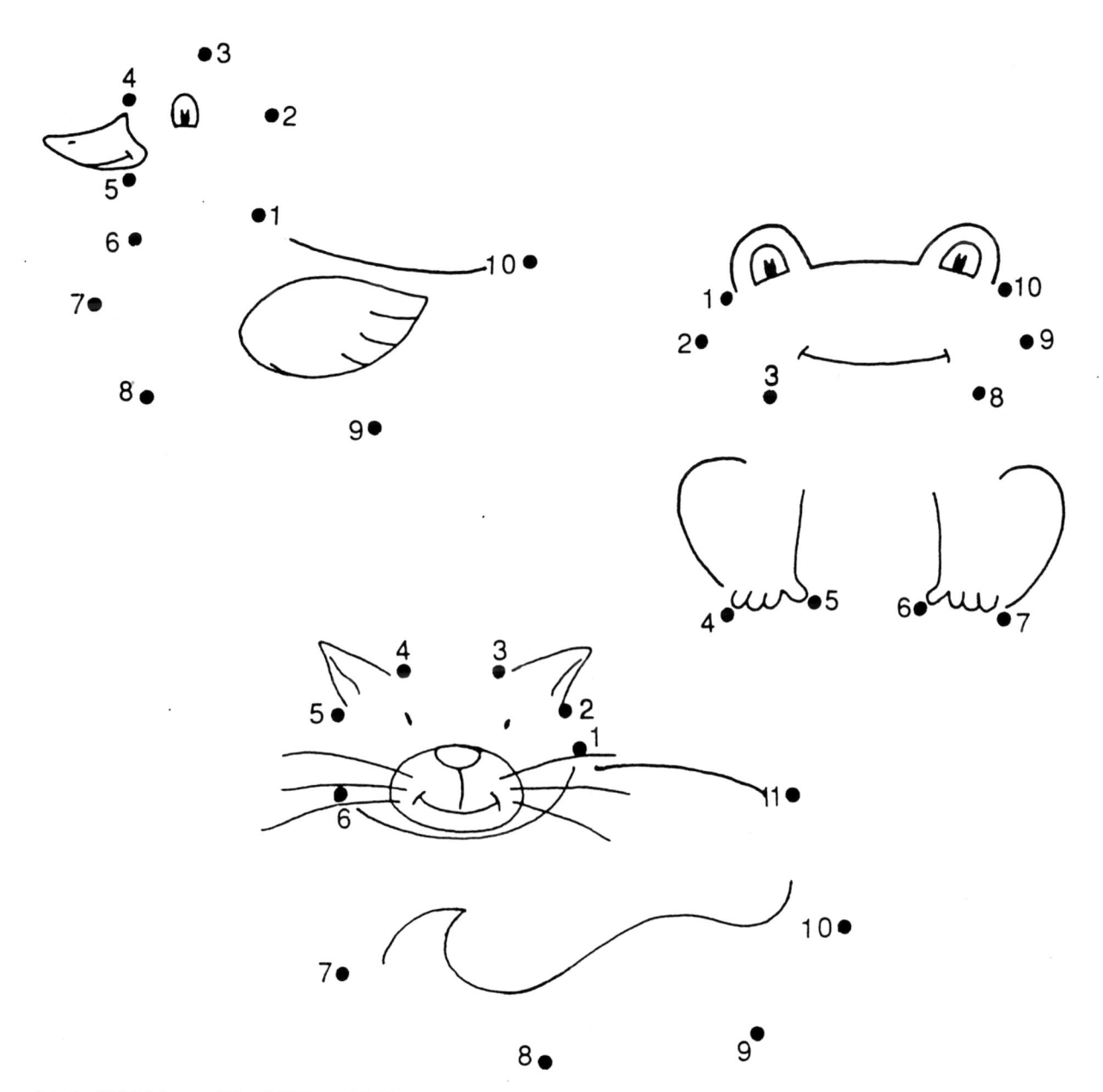

Snow White

Find the missing numbers

Flowers

Colour the flowers with 3 petals red.
Colour the flowers with 4 petals blue.
Colour the flowers with 5 petals purple.
Colour the centres yellow and the leaves and stems green.

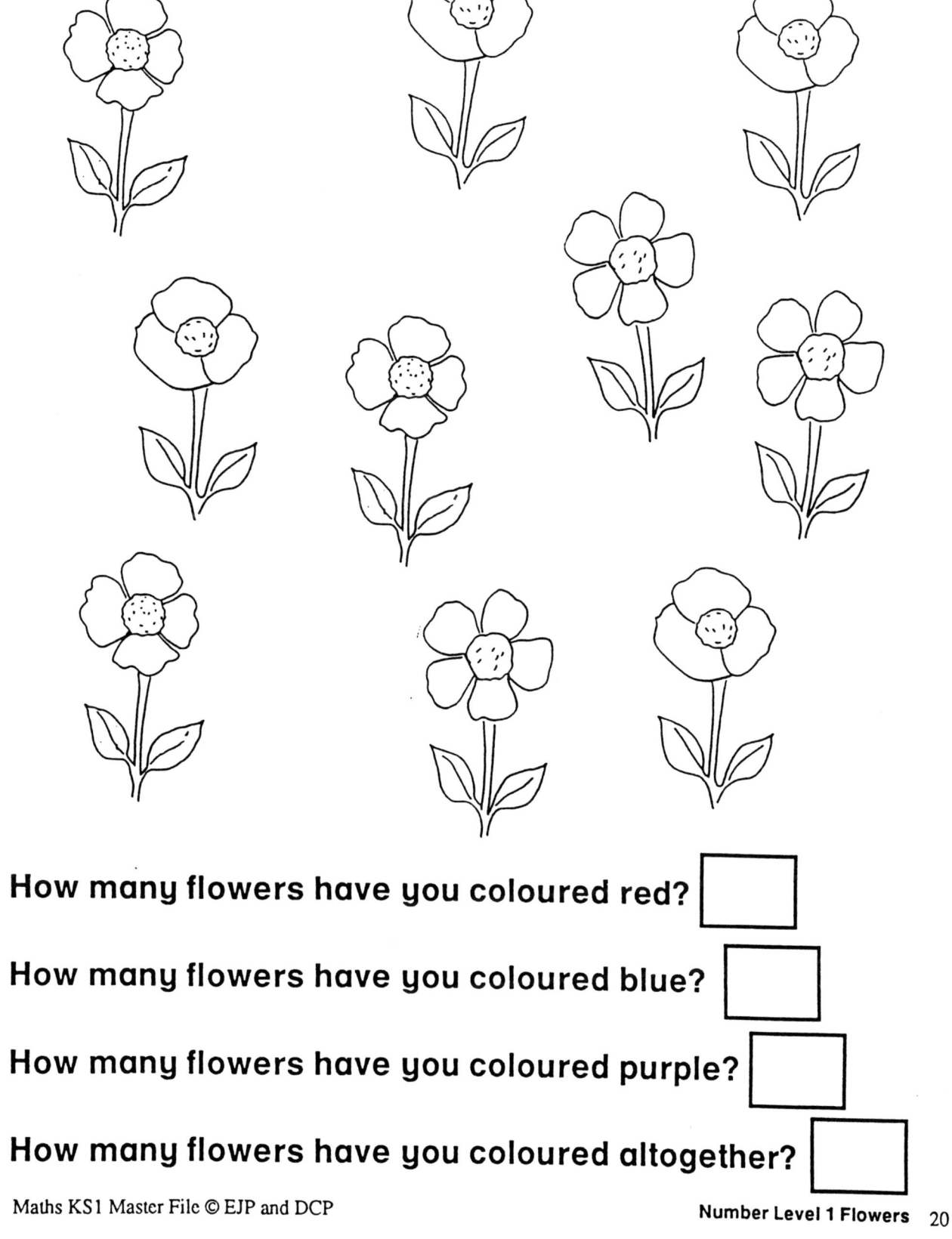

How many flowers have you coloured red?

How many flowers have you coloured blue?

How many flowers have you coloured purple?

How many flowers have you coloured altogether?

Conservation of numbers

Colour and count.

Colour sets of 2 green, sets of 3 red, sets of 4 blue and sets of 5 yellow.

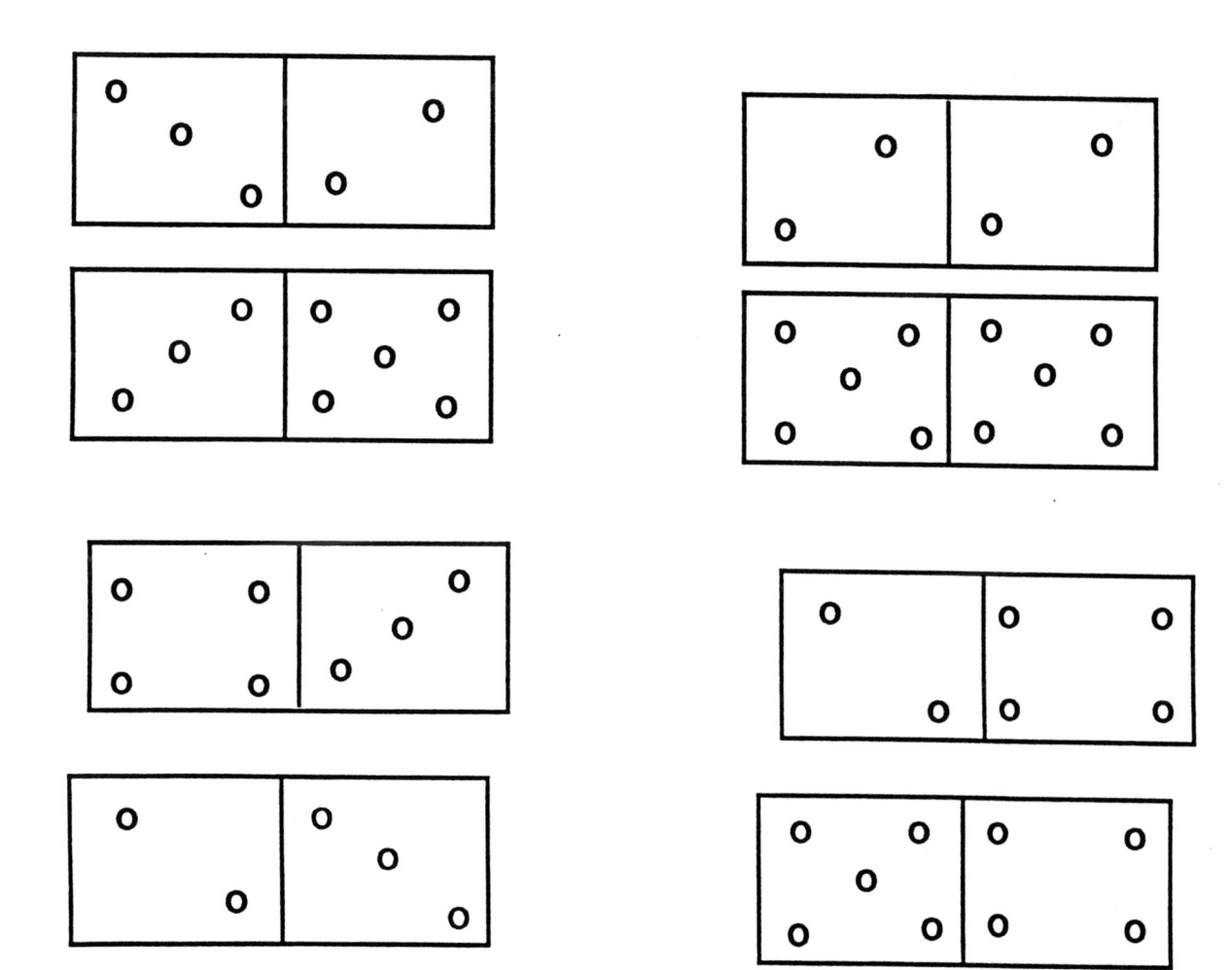

Maths KS1 Master File © EJP and DCP

Number Level 1 Conservation of Numbers 21

Addition

Draw and colour 1 more. How many now?

Draw and colour 2 more. How many now?

Draw and colour 3 more. How many now?

Draw and colour 4 more. How many now?

Draw and colour 5 more. How many now?

Draw and colour 6 more. How many now?

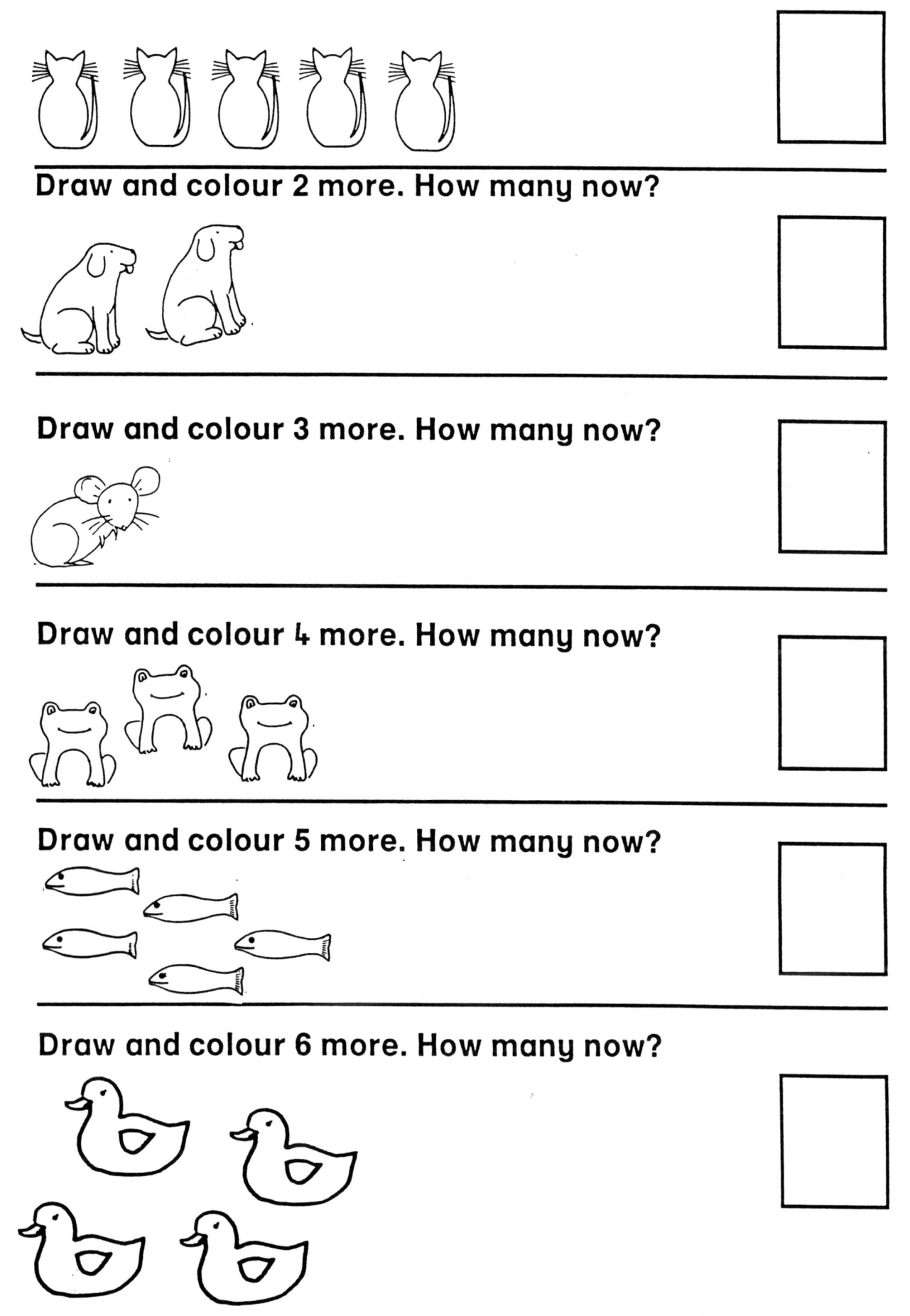

Add

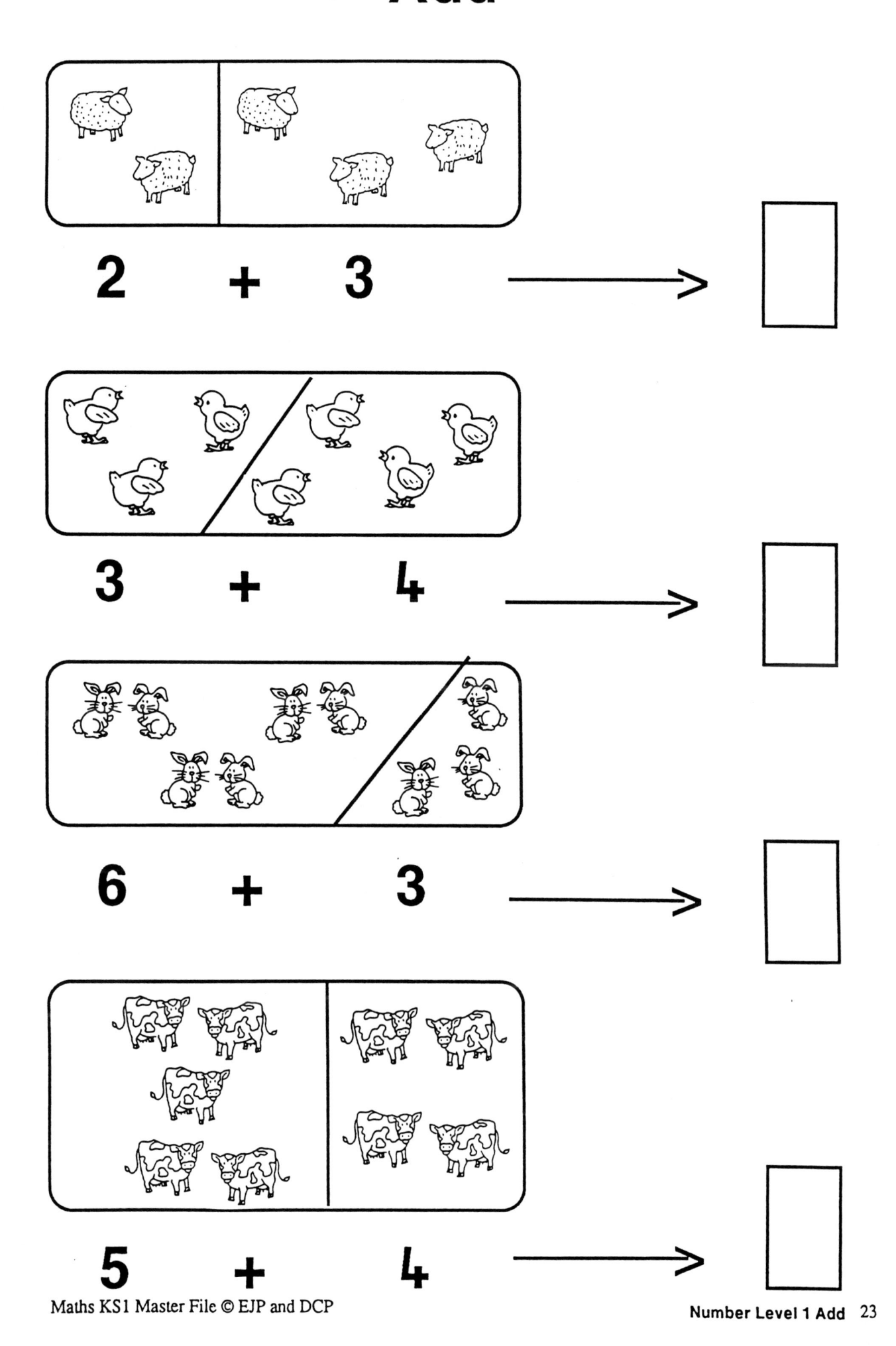

2 + 3 ⟶ ☐

3 + 4 ⟶ ☐

6 + 3 ⟶ ☐

5 + 4 ⟶ ☐

Make 5

Paste on thin board. Colour and cut out the cards. Put the cards together to make sets of 5.

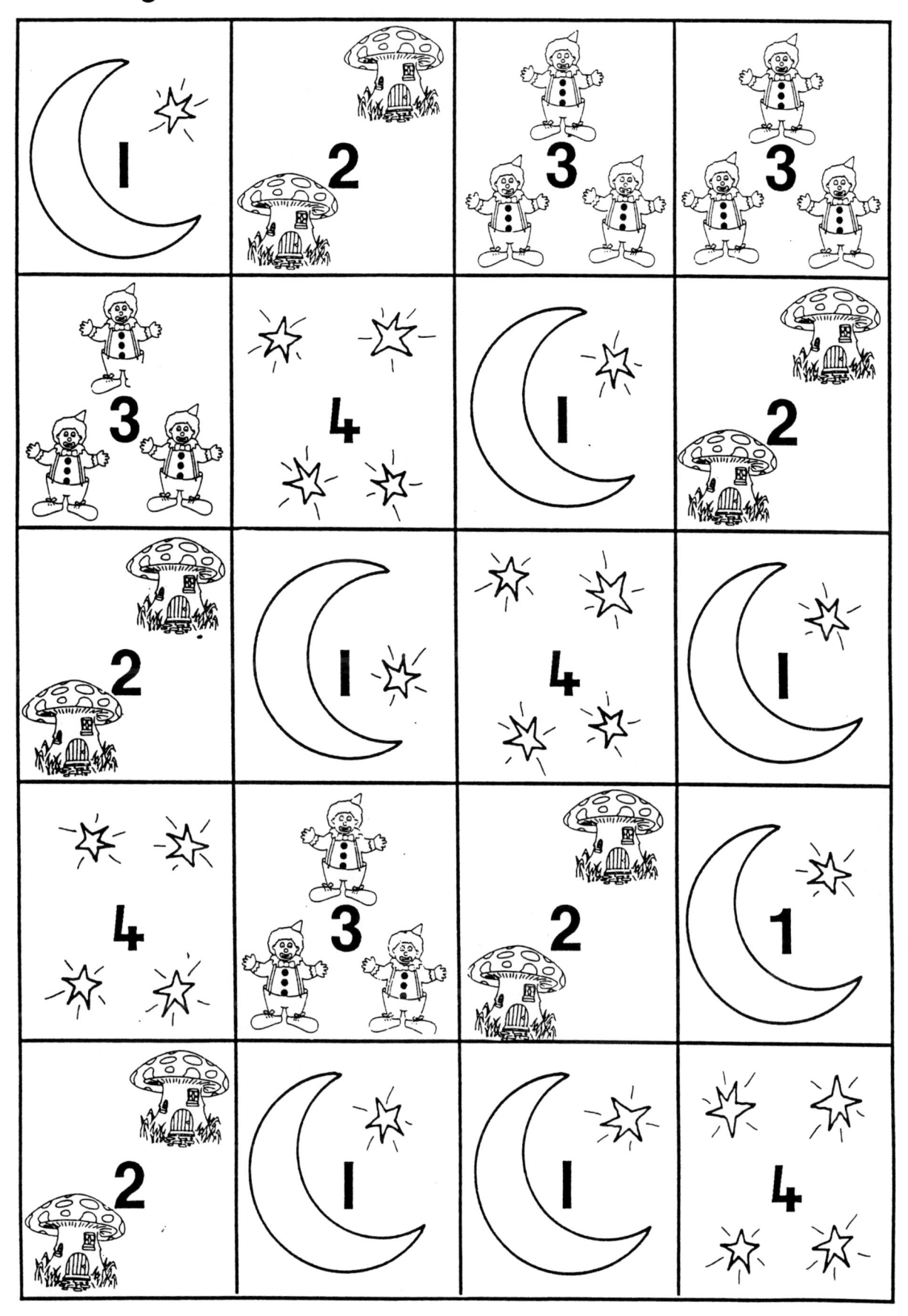

Maths KS1 Master File © EJP and DCP

Number Level 2 Make 5 24

Make 10

Paste on thin board. Colour and cut out the cards. Put the cards together to make sets of 10.

2	1	6	7
8	2	4	5
1	5	2	3
3	6	8	4
7	4	3	9

Maths KS1 Master File © EJP and DCP

Number Level 2 Make 10 25

How many leaves?

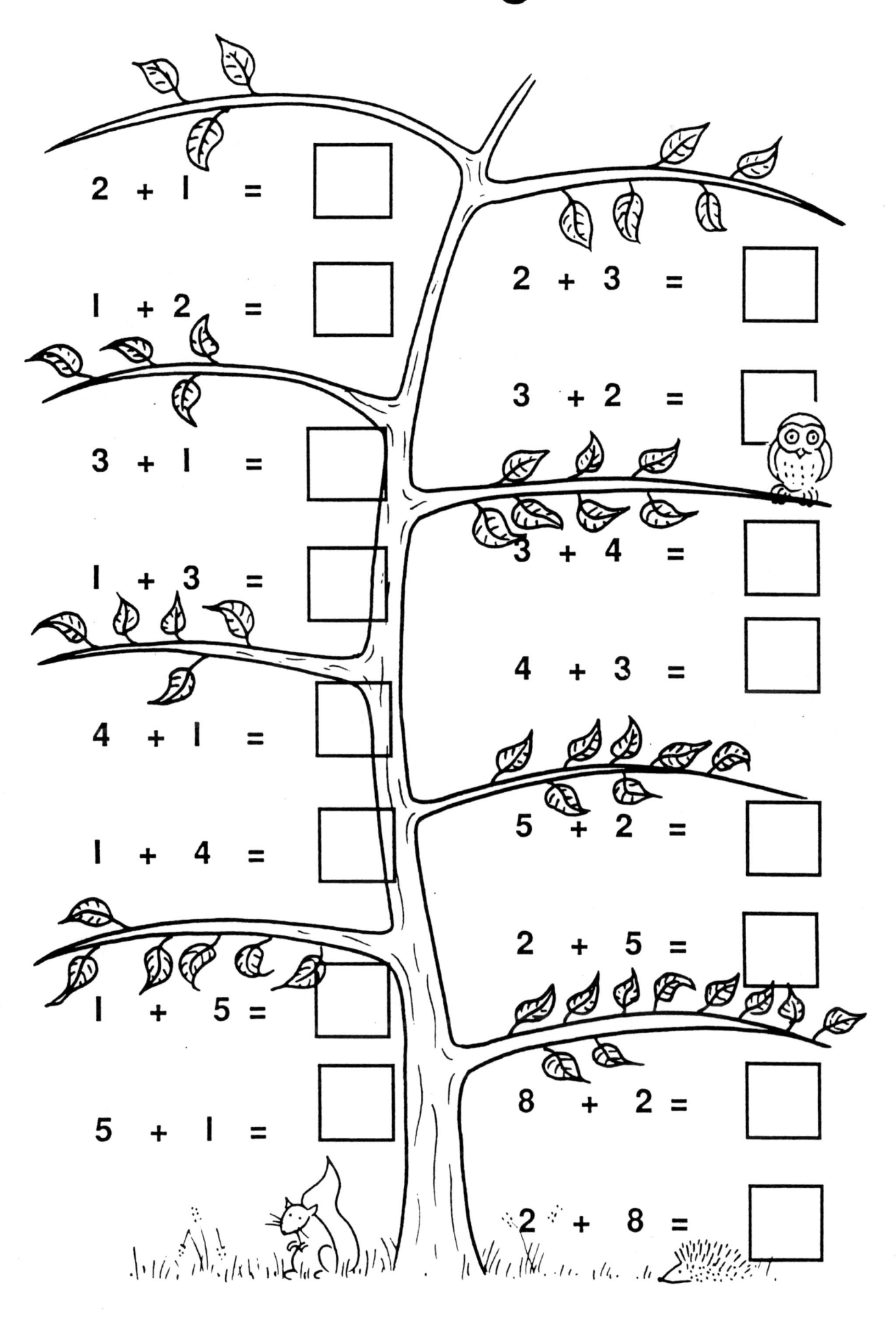

2 + 1 = ☐

1 + 2 = ☐

3 + 1 = ☐

1 + 3 = ☐

4 + 1 = ☐

1 + 4 = ☐

1 + 5 = ☐

5 + 1 = ☐

2 + 3 = ☐

3 + 2 = ☐

3 + 4 = ☐

4 + 3 = ☐

5 + 2 = ☐

2 + 5 = ☐

8 + 2 = ☐

2 + 8 = ☐

Take away strips

Take away 1. How many are left?

Take away 2. How many are left?

Take away 3. How many are left?

Take away 5. How many are left?

Take away 7. How many are left?

Take away 8. How many are left?

Take away 9. How many are left?

Maths KS1 Master File © EJP and DCP

Subtraction

How many apples are there? ☐

2 are eaten. How many are left? ☐

How many bones are there? ☐

Spot runs away with one. How many are left? ☐

Find the missing numbers.

5 - 4 ☐   6 - 2 ☐   3 - 1 ☐   6 - 4 ☐

10 - 3 ☐   9 - 5 ☐   8 - 5 ☐   5 - 3 ☐

6 - 5 ☐   3 - 2 ☐   4 - 3 ☐   7 - 2 ☐

9 - 5 ☐   8 - 3 ☐   9 - 8 ☐   8 - 7 ☐

Add or subtract

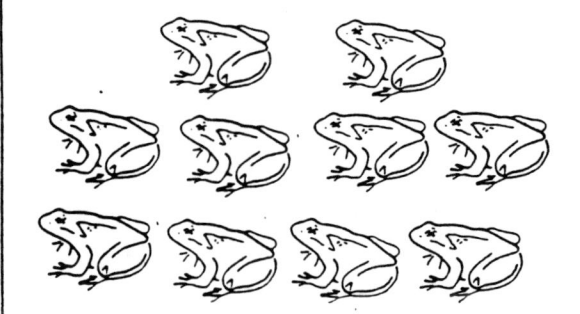

3 + 1 =	3 - 2 =
2 + 2 =	4 - 3 =
4 + 2 =	6 - 1 =
2 + 5 =	5 - 3 =
6 + 1 =	8 - 2 =
3 + 4 =	9 - 6 =
2 + 8 =	7 - 3 =
9 + 1 =	6 - 2 =
1 + 4 =	5 - 4 =
7 + 2 =	9 - 5 =

Add

How many children are on the bus?

5
+
3

8

1 + 2	3 + 1	2 + 3	2 + 0	5 + 4	1
4 + 3	3 + 5	8 + 1	0 + 8	3 + 6	2 3 4 5
2 + 2	2 + 8	3 + 3	6 + 0	7 + 2	6 7 8
3 + 4	2 + 5	8 + 1	9 + 0	4 + 2	9 10

Take away

If 2 children get off the bus, how many are left on the bus?

8
−
2

6

2−	3−	3−	2−	5−
1	1	2	0	4

8−	5−	9−	3−	6−
1	3	1	3	4

2−	8−	5−	6−	7−
2	2	5	0	2

7−	9−	8−	9−	1−
4	5	1	0	1

1
2
3
4
5
6
7
8
9
10

Find the missing numbers

There were 3 cakes, now there is 1. How many cakes have been eaten?

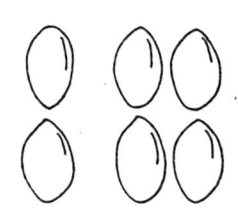

1 + ☐ = 3

Jane dropped the box of 6 eggs. How many were broken?

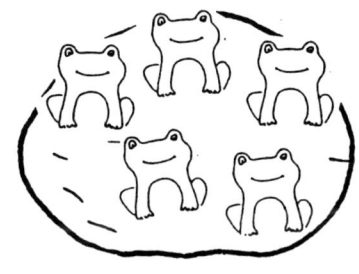

2 + ☐ = 6

There were 9 frogs hiding under this stone. 5 came out. How many frogs are still hiding?

☐ + 5 = 9

There were 5 apples on the tree. Now there are 2. How many apples have fallen off the tree?

5 - ☐ = 2

Some more missing numbers for you to find.

3 + ☐ = 4

5 - ☐ = 3

4 + ☐ = 7

☐ + 2 = 6

☐ - 3 = 4

9 - 2 = ☐

Estimate

Estimate how many things there are then count them.

stars

estimate about ☐   count ☐

raindrops

estimate about ☐   count ☐

sheep

estimate about ☐   count ☐

cars

estimate about ☐   count ☐

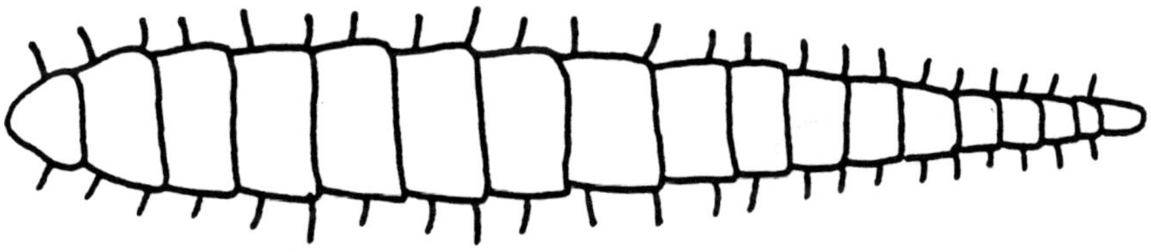

legs

estimate about ☐   count ☐

Maths KS1 Master File © EJP and DCP

Left luggage

Write the missing numbers.

21	22		24		26	27			30
31		33		35			38		
	42			45		47		49	

Draw the pictures where they belong in these left luggage lockers. Number 43 has been done for you.

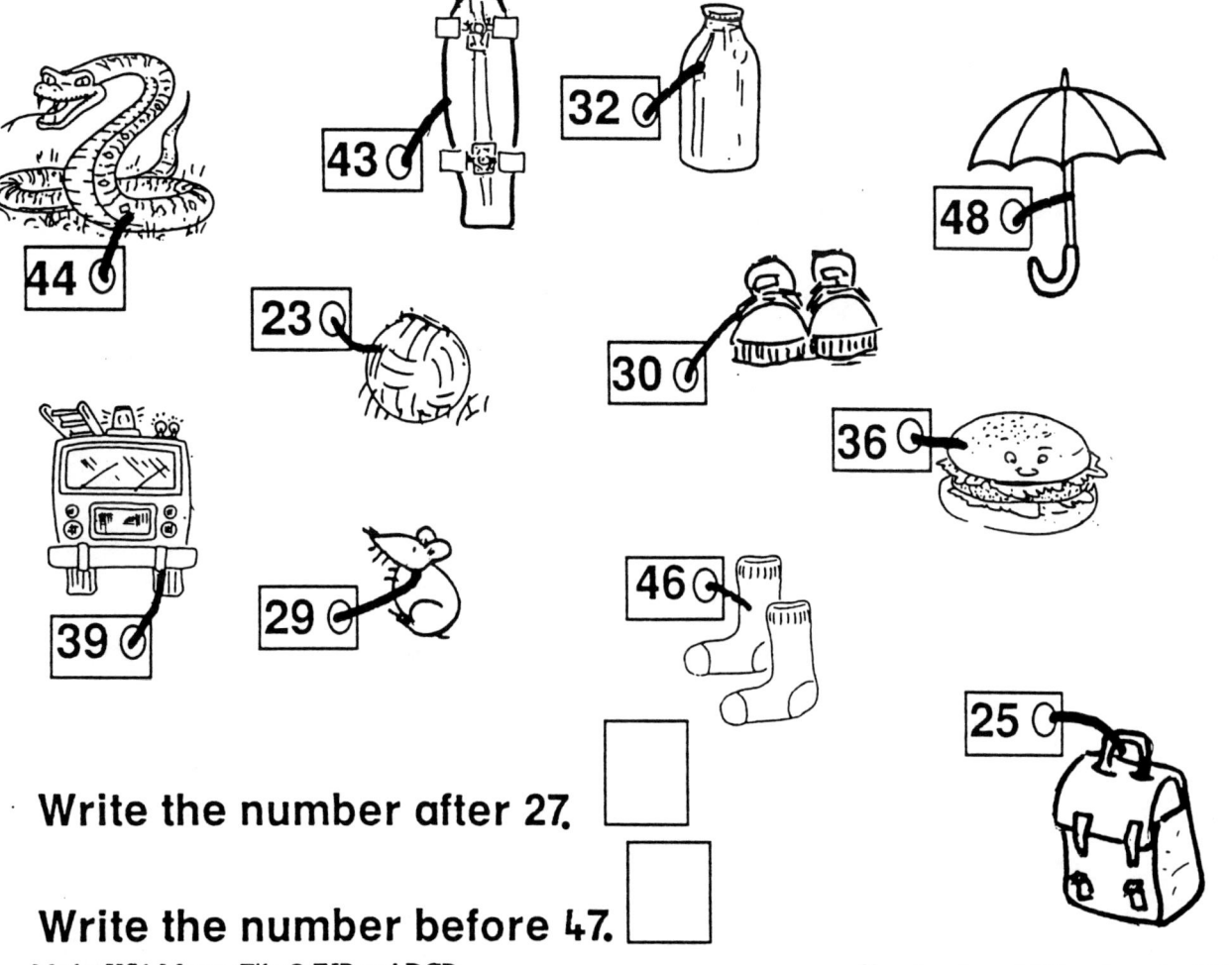

Write the number after 27. ☐

Write the number before 47. ☐

Ordering

Colour the first and third sheep blue.
Colour the rest orange.

Colour the second and fourth dogs brown.
Colour the rest black.

Colour the first, middle and last snakes green.
Colour the others red.

How many are there in each set?

Tick the one with the most.

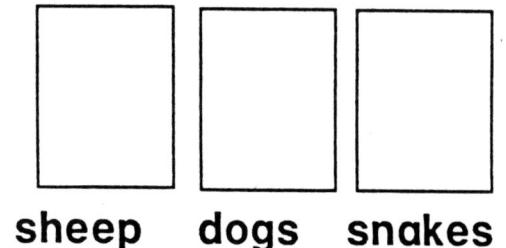

sheep   dogs   snakes

Now try this.

76   91   10   44   19   9   38   82   50   67

Write these numbers in order beginning with the smallest and ending with the biggest.

Catch a falling star

Meet Sam, the astronaut. Colour the game sheet. 2 players need 15 stars or counters, 3 players need 12. Throw a die to decide who goes first. When it is your turn, use three of your stars or counters to cover three numbers anywhere on the board that add up to 10. Each star on the board can be any number you like but you must say what the number is. The winner is the player who uses all his or her stars or counters first.

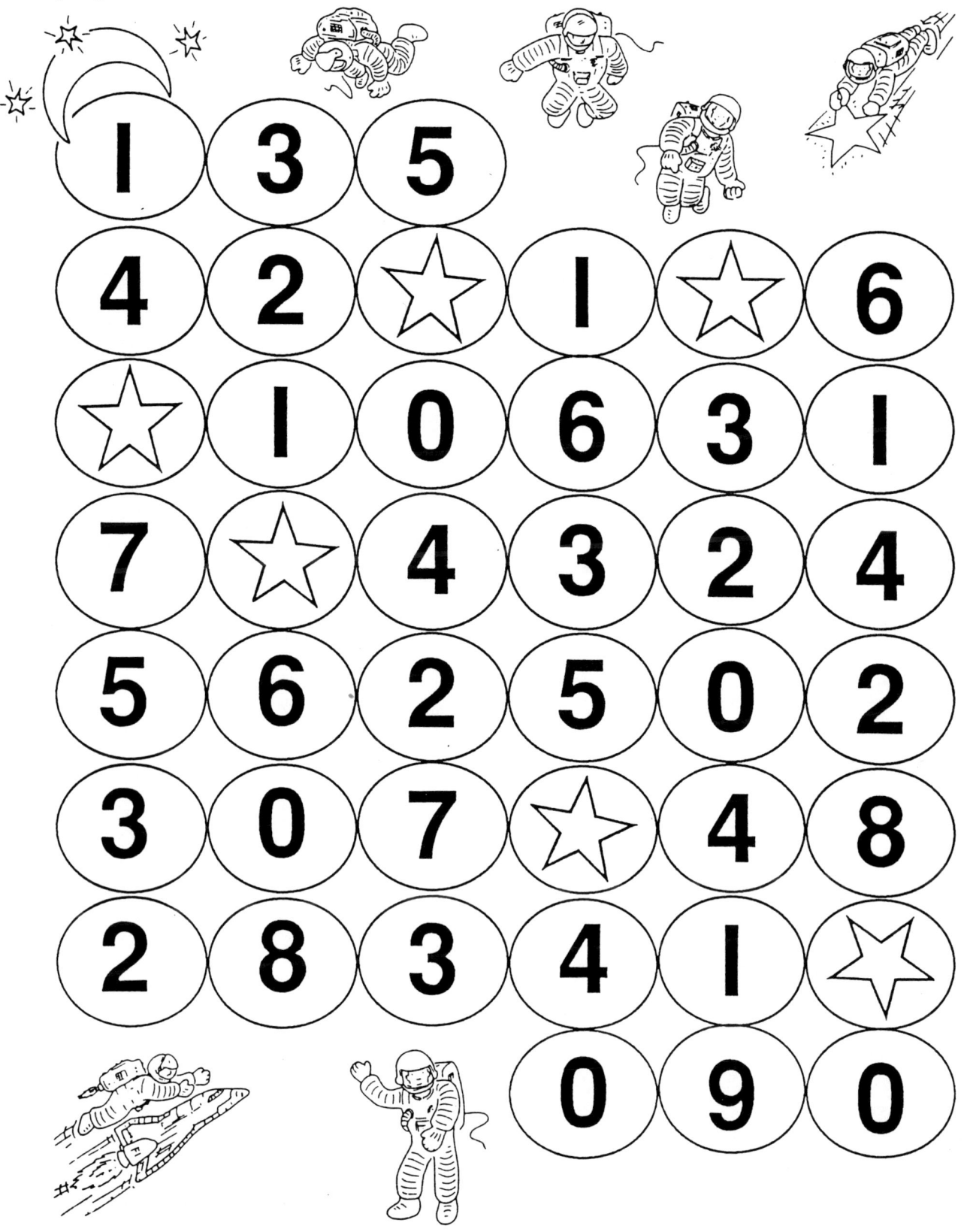

1	3	5			
4	2	☆	1	☆	6
☆	1	0	6	3	1
7	☆	4	3	2	4
5	6	2	5	0	2
3	0	7	☆	4	8
2	8	3	4	1	☆
			0	9	0

Maths KS1 Master File © EJP and DCP   Number Level 2 Catch a Falling Star 36

Money

Join the purses which contain the same amounts of money.

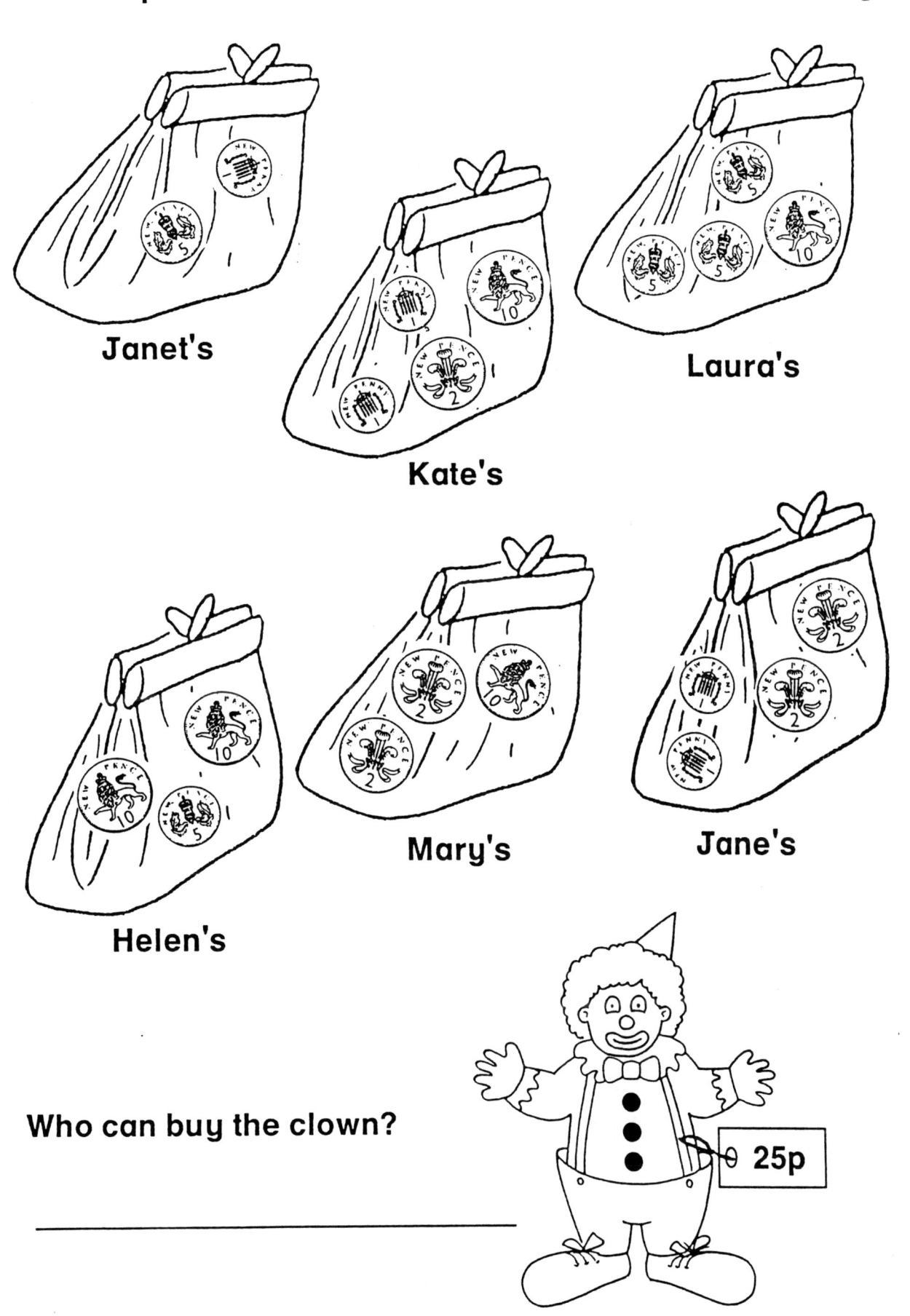

Janet's (5p, 5p)

Kate's (5p, 10p, 1p, 2p)

Laura's (5p, 5p, 5p, 10p)

Helen's (10p, 10p, 5p)

Mary's (2p, 2p, 2p)

Jane's (1p, 2p, 2p, 2p)

Who can buy the clown? 25p

_____

Maths KS1 Master File © EJP and DCP   Number Level 2 Money 37

Shopping

Choose any 3 of these coins to buy the things below.

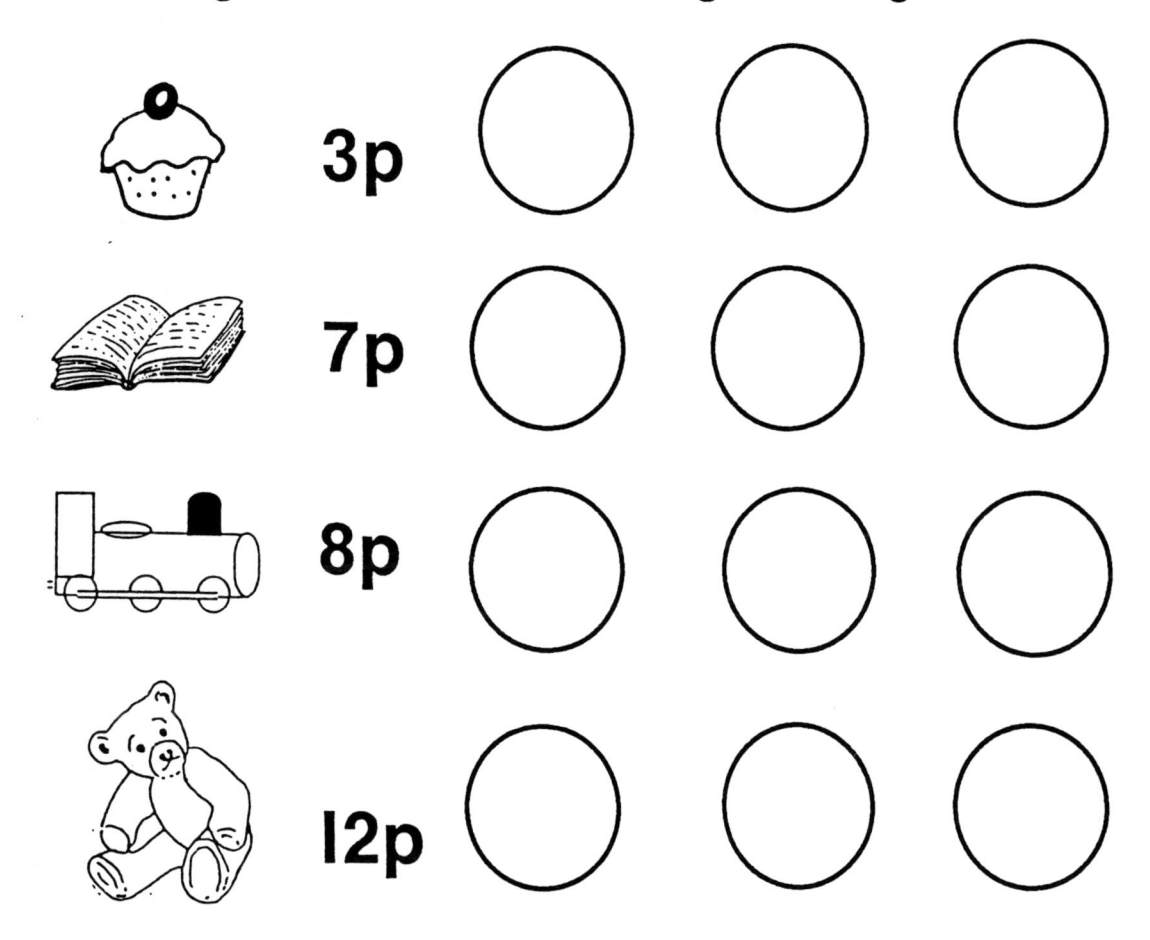

3p	○	○	○
7p	○	○	○
8p	○	○	○
12p	○	○	○

Peter buys a pencil for 4p and pays with a 5p coin. How much change does he get?

Jane buys an ice cream for 8p and pays with a 10p coin. How much change does she get?

John has 15p and wants to buy a book for 17p. How much more money does he need?

Car boot sale

Here are some things you might bring to sell or buy. Price cards are at the bottom of the page. Don't forget to barter and to look out for special bargains. Some are blank for you to draw.

dinosaur	doll	cakes	boat	train
apples	an alien	clown	rugby ball	bucket and spade
dragon	teddy	crayons		

1p   3p   4p

BARGAINS   10p   20p

Maths KS1 Master File © EJP and DCP

Number Level 2 Shopping 39

Half ($\frac{1}{2}$)

Colour half of each shape red.

Draw a line to divide this cake into two halves.

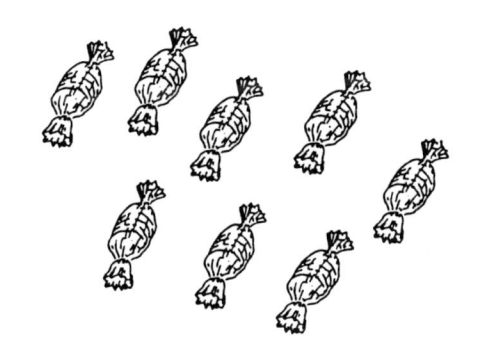

Divide these sweets into 2 equal groups.

Divide these ducks into 2 equal groups. Colour each group a different colour.

Quarter ($\frac{1}{4}$)

Colour quarter of this cake green.

Colour quarter of this butterfly red.

Colour quarter of this square orange.

Colour quarter of the petals of this flower pink.

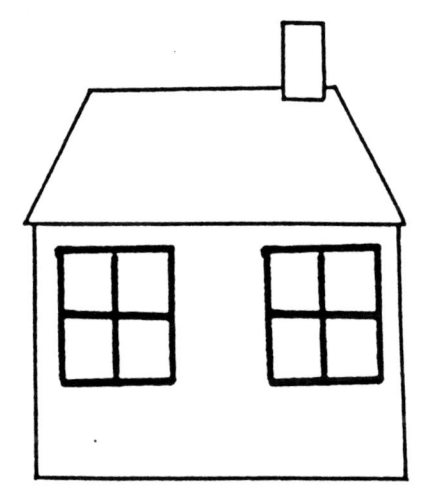

Colour a quarter of each window blue.

Divide these sweets into 4 equal groups. Colour each group a different colour.

Divide these chicks into 4 equal groups. Colour each group a different colour.

Measuring

Measure the top of a table using your handspan. How many?

Measure the height of a chair using your handspan. How many?

Measure the length of the classroom using strides. How many?

Guess how many strides it will take you to walk around the school playground.

How many?

Then count your strides as you walk around the playground.

How many?

Was your guess close?

Why do people get different answers?

Measuring

Colour the shortest person green.
Colour the tallest person blue.
Colour the fattest person red.

Which is the heavier object?
Draw a line from the objects to the correct scales.

Make a chart for yourself.

Age	Name
Height	cm
Weight	kg

Drawing of me.

Measures

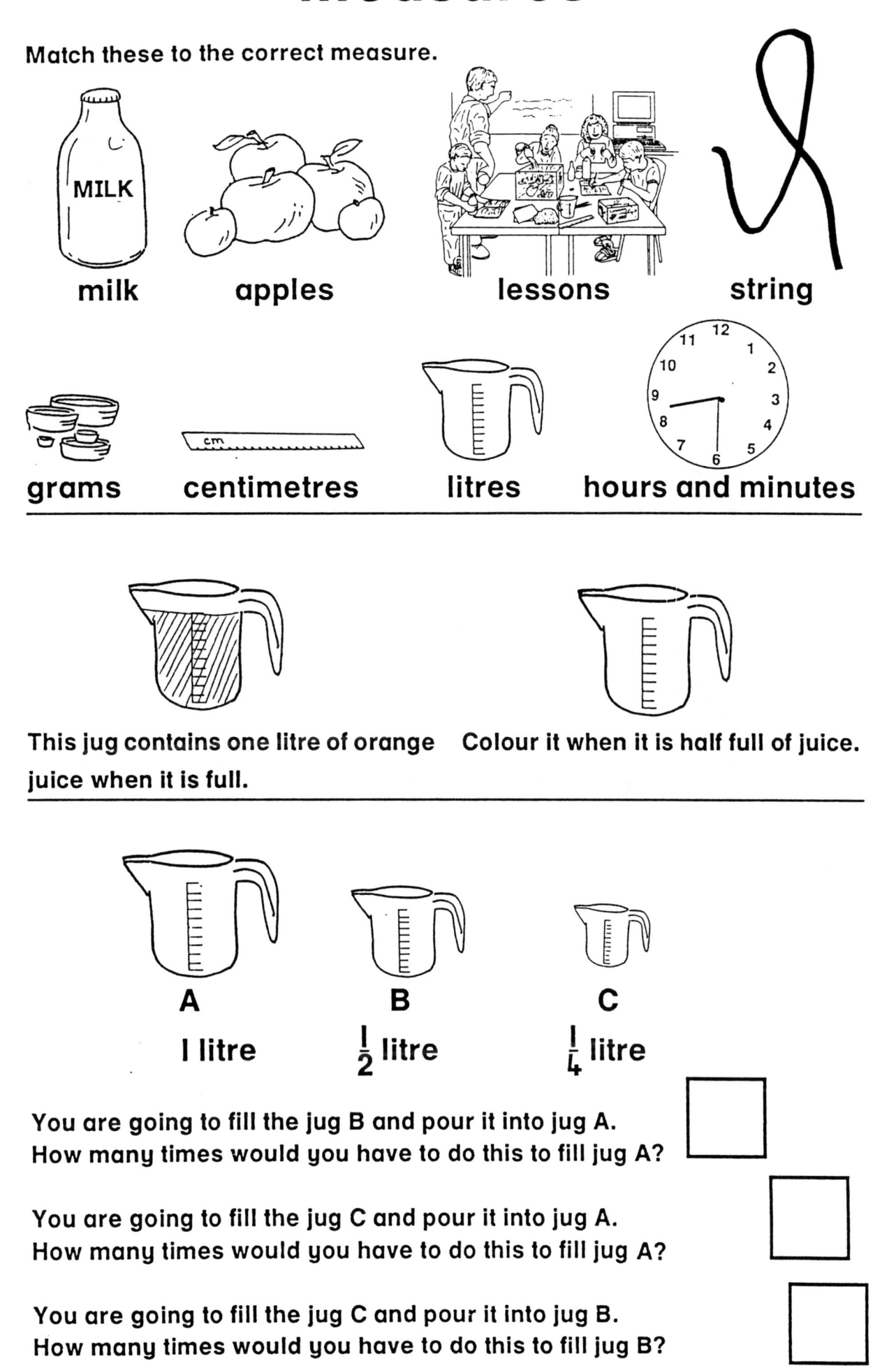

Match these to the correct measure.

milk   apples   lessons   string

grams   centimetres   litres   hours and minutes

This jug contains one litre of orange juice when it is full.

Colour it when it is half full of juice.

A — 1 litre
B — ½ litre
C — ¼ litre

You are going to fill the jug B and pour it into jug A.
How many times would you have to do this to fill jug A?

You are going to fill the jug C and pour it into jug A.
How many times would you have to do this to fill jug A?

You are going to fill the jug C and pour it into jug B.
How many times would you have to do this to fill jug B?

Patterns

Colour the small squares then fill the big square with the pattern.

red	blue	red	blue
blue	red		
red			

Colour the beads and then draw the next 3 beads.

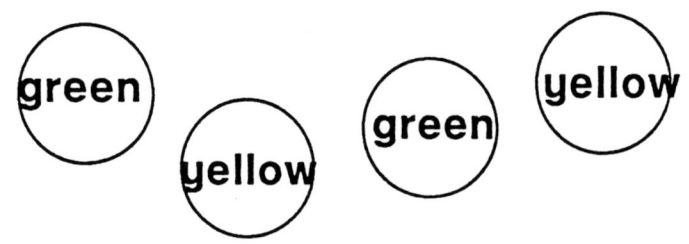

green   yellow   green   yellow

Draw the next 3 shapes in this pattern.

Write the next 3 numbers.

1 2 3   1 2 3   1 _____

Write the next 3 letters

a   c   e _____

Number bonds

Find the missing numbers.

Make 2	Make 3	Make 4	Make 5
0 + 2	0 + 3	0 + 4	0 + 5
1 + 1	1 + 2	1 + 3	1 + 4
2 +	2 +	2 +	2 +
	3 +	3 +	3 +
		4 +	4 +
			5 +

Make 6	Make 7	Make 8	Make 9
0 + 6	0 + 7	0 +	0 +
1 + 5	1 + 6	1 +	1 +
2 +	2 +	2 +	2 +
3 +	3 +	3 +	3 +
4 +	4 +	4 +	4 +
5 +	5 +	5 +	5 +
6 +	6 +	6 +	6 +
	7 +	7 +	7 +
		8 +	8 +
			9 +

Make 10	Make 2	Make 5	Make 7
0 +	2 − 0	5 − 0	7 −
1 +	3 − 1	6 − 1	8 −
2 +	4 − 2	7 −	9 −
3 +	5 −	8 −	10 −
4 +	6 −	9 −	
5 +	7 −	10 −	
6 +	8 −		
7 +	9 −		
8 +	10 −		
9 +			
10 +			

Odds and evens

Tick the correct boxes.
Colour the biscuits red and yellow.
Is there an odd or even
number of biscuits on this plate?

Odd ☐   Even ☐

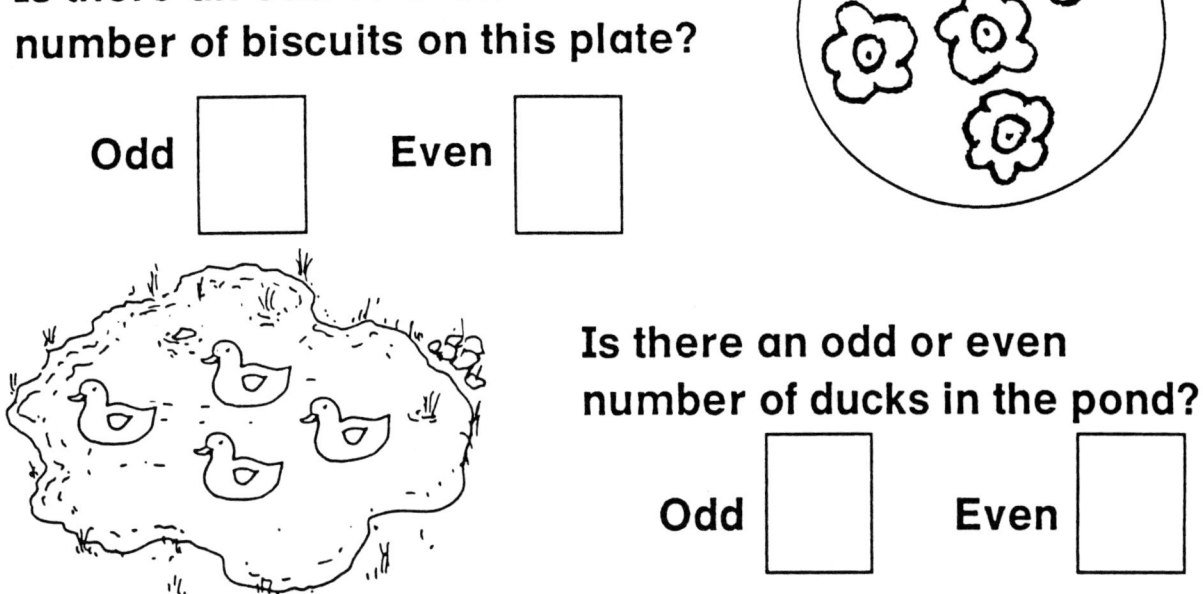

Is there an odd or even
number of ducks in the pond?

Odd ☐   Even ☐

Write all the odd numbers between 4 and 21

_____

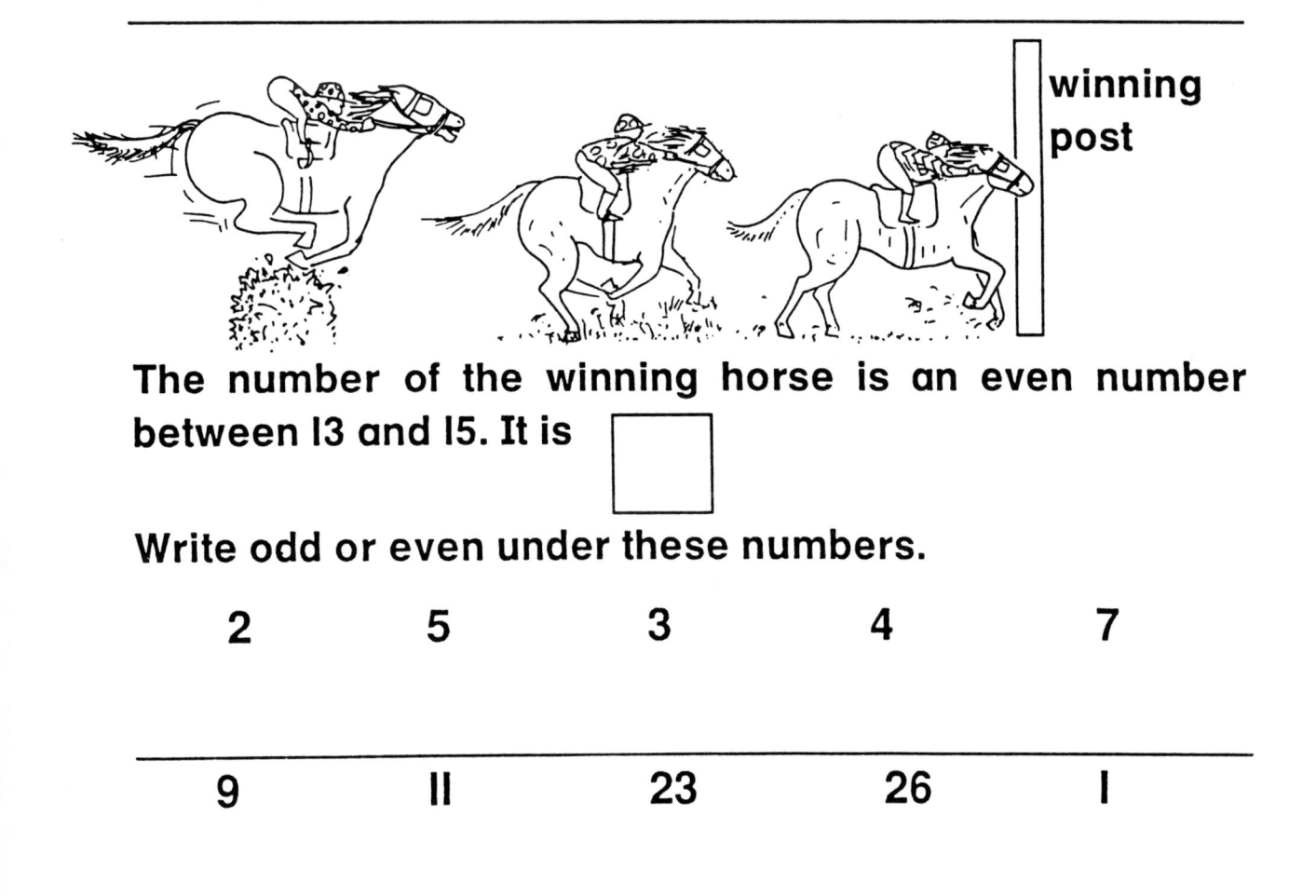

The number of the winning horse is an even number between 13 and 15. It is ☐

Write odd or even under these numbers.

| 2 | 5 | 3 | 4 | 7 |

| 9 | 11 | 23 | 26 | 1 |

An add 3 robot

Find the numbers that come out.

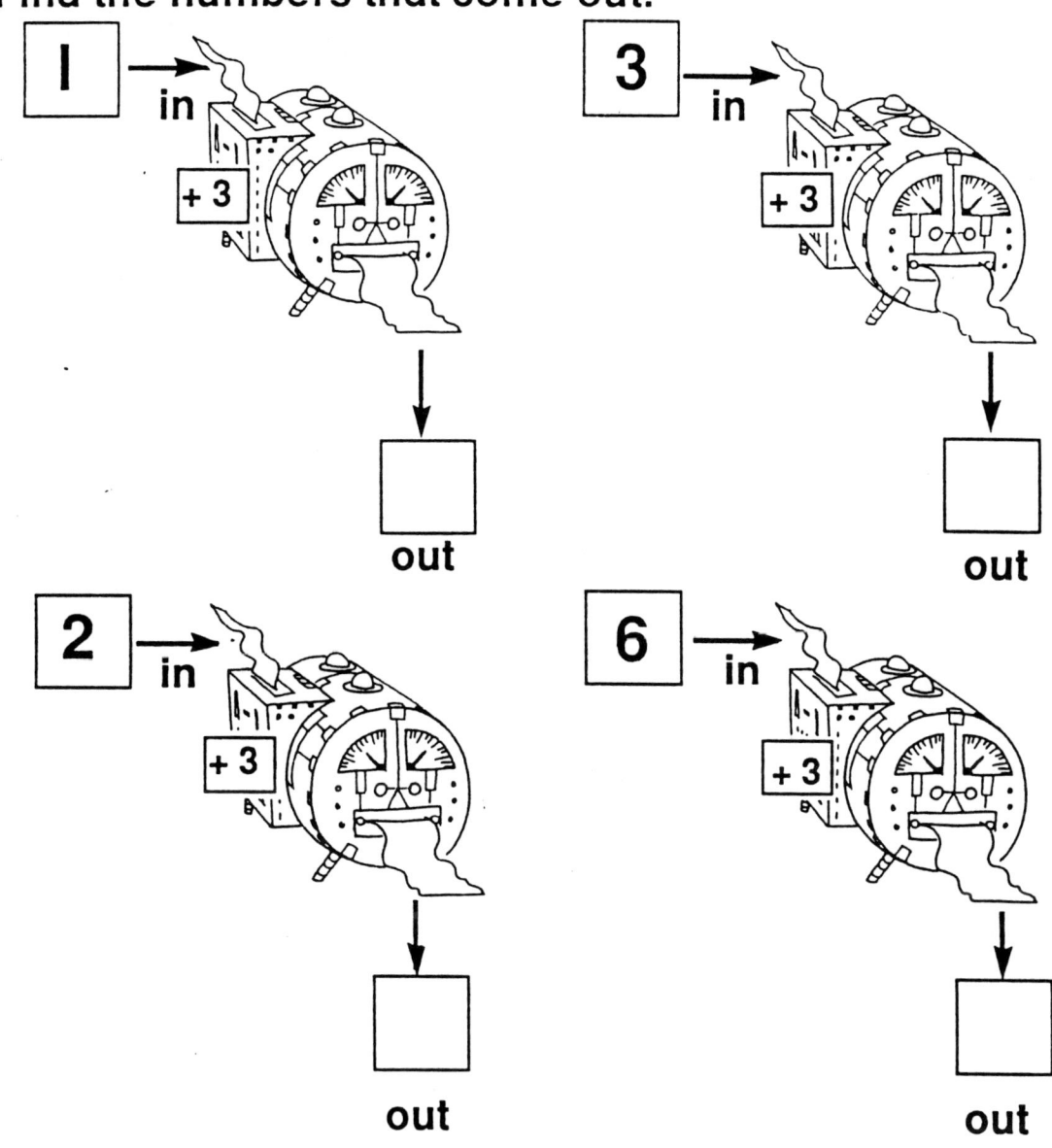

| in: 1, +3, out: ☐ | in: 3, +3, out: ☐ |
| in: 2, +3, out: ☐ | in: 6, +3, out: ☐ |

Find the numbers that go in.

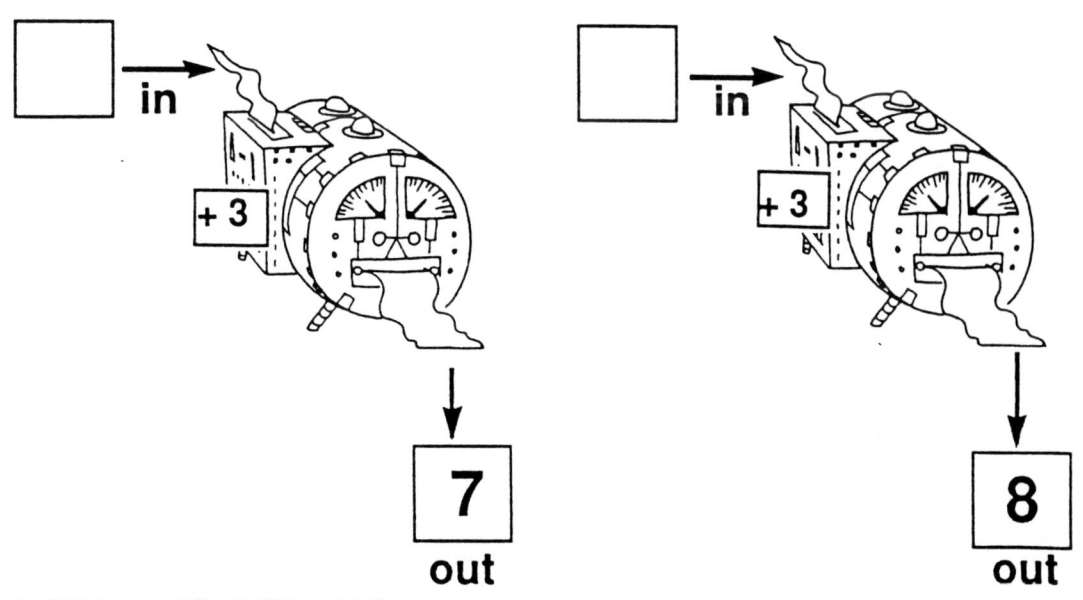

| in: ☐, +3, out: 7 | in: ☐, +3, out: 8 |

A take away 4 robot

Find the numbers that come out.

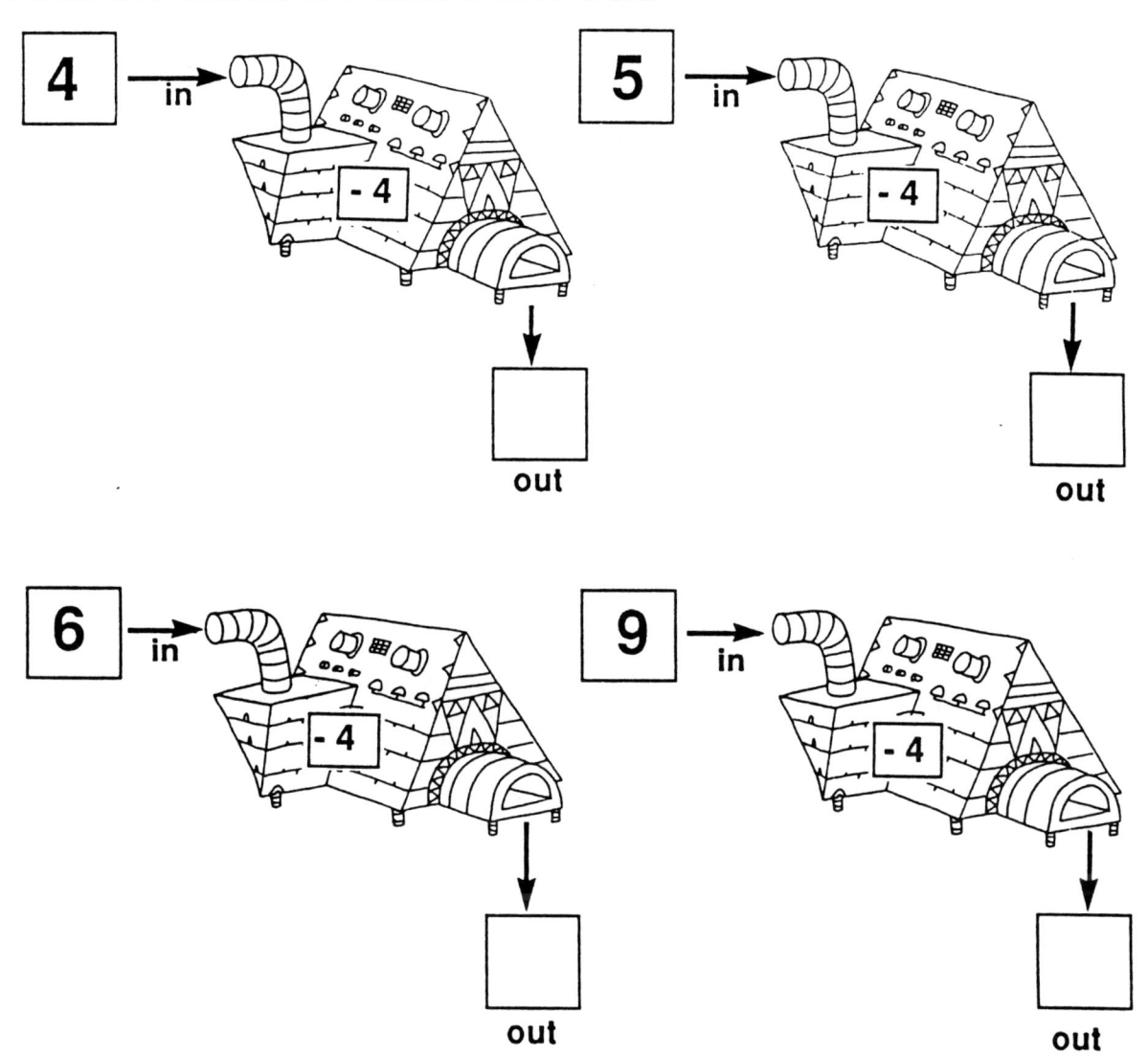

4 in → [−4] → out ☐

5 in → [−4] → out ☐

6 in → [−4] → out ☐

9 in → [−4] → out ☐

Find the numbers that go in.

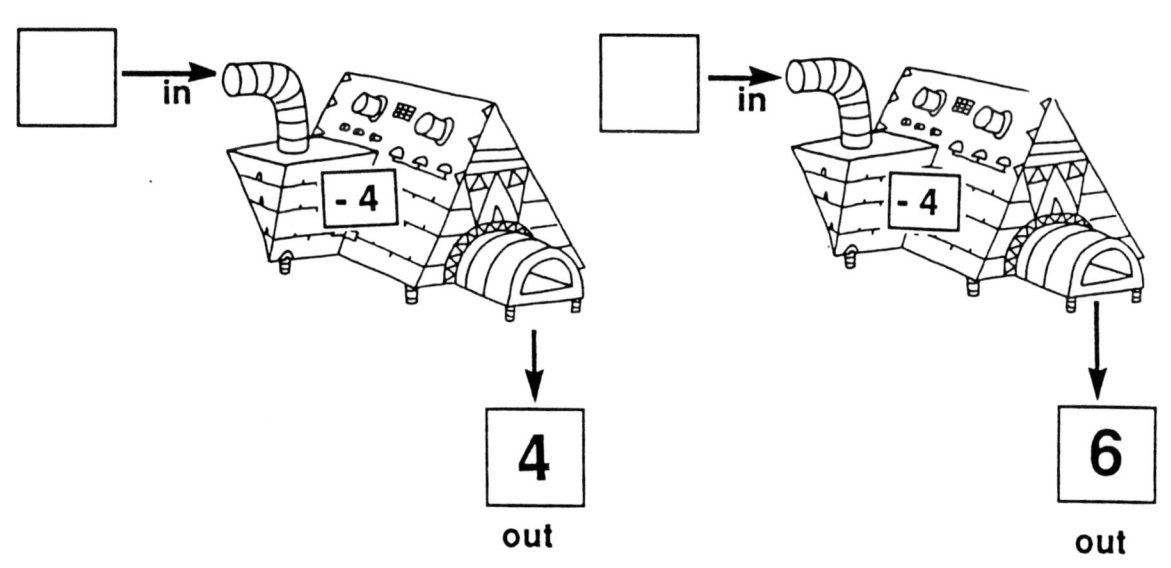

☐ in → [−4] → out 4

☐ in → [−4] → out 6

Maths KS1 Master File © EJP and DCP

Multiplication and counting on

Find the missing numbers.

X 2

0 x 2 = 0
1 x 2 =
2 x 2 =
3 x 2 =
4 x 2 =
5 x 2 =
6 x 2 =
7 x 2 =
8 x 2 =
9 x 2 =
10 x 2 =

counting in 2s

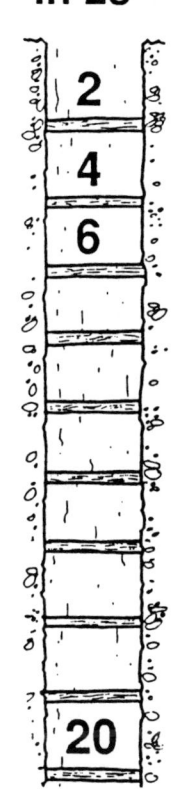

2
4
6
20

X 3

0 x 3 = 0
1 x 3 =
2 x 3 =
3 x 3 =
4 x 3 =
5 x 3 =
6 x 3 =
7 x 3 =
8 x 3 =
9 x 3 =
10 x 3 =

counting in 3s

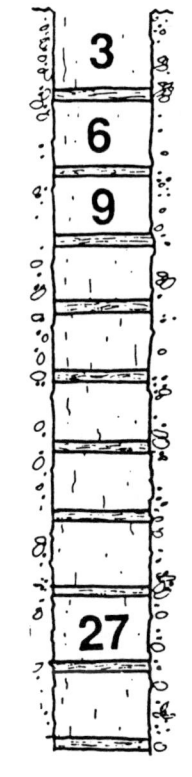

3
6
9
27

X 5

0 x 5 = 0
1 x 5 =
2 x 5 =
3 x 5 =
4 x 5 =
5 x 5 =
6 x 5 =
7 x 5 =
8 x 5 =
9 x 5 =
10 x 5 =

counting in 5s

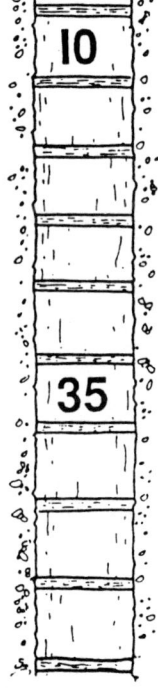

5
10
35

X 10

0 x 10 = 0
1 x 10 =
2 x 10 =
3 x 10 =
4 x 10 =
5 x 10 =
6 x 10 =
7 x 10 =
8 x 10 =
9 x 10 =
10 x 10 =

counting in 10s

10
20
60

Maths KS1 Master File © EJP and DCP

2, 5 and 10

This is part of a hundred number square.

1	2	3	4	5	6	7	8	9	10
11	12	13	14	15	16	17	18	19	20
21	22	23	24	25	26	27	28	29	30
31	32	33	34	35	36	37	38	39	40
41	42	43	44	45	46	47	48	49	50

Colour yellow all the squares that can be divided exactly by 2.

Draw a blue cross on all the squares that can be divided exactly by 5.

Draw a red circle on all the squares that can be divided exactly by 10.

Write the numbers between 27 and 37 that can be divided exactly by 2.

_____

Write the numbers in the square that can be divided exactly by 5.

_____

Write the numbers in the square that can be divided exactly by 10.

_____

20 can be divided exactly by 2, 5 and 10. Write the other numbers in the square which can be divided exactly by 2, 5 and 10.

_____

Which numbers in the square can be divided exactly by 5 but not by 2?

_____

Which numbers in the square can be divided exactly by 5 but not by 10?

_____

Multiply squares

Find the missing numbers in these multiply squares. The first one has been done for you.

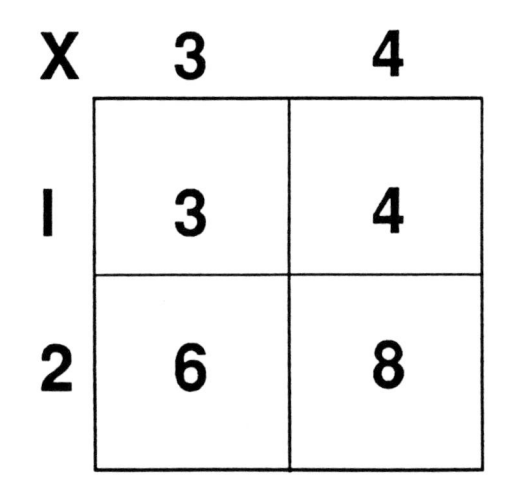

X	3	4
1	3	4
2	6	8

X	2	3
1		
2		

X	4	5
2		
3		

X	2	5
2		
10		

X	3	
1		4
2		

X		5
1	1	
2		

Maths KS1 Master File © EJP and DCP   Number Level 3 Multiply Squares 52

Bingo (multiplication)

Paste the bingo and caller cards on to cardboard and cut out. Mix the caller cards and place in a pile face down. Choose a caller. The caller turns over the cards one at a time and calls out the numbers. The children cover the numbers on their bingo cards which have the same answer as the number called. For example, if 10 is called then 5 x 2 and 10 x 1 are covered. The winners are those who cover their bingo card first. The class can make their own bingo cards.

3 x 2	4 x 5	2 x 10
5 x 5	0 x 3	5 x 2

4 x 2	3 x 10	2 x 5
7 x 10	5 x 3	3 x 3

9 x 10	6 x 5	4 x 10
3 x 5	8 x 2	7 x 3

7 x 2	8 x 5	8 x 3
9 x 3	5 x 10	10 x 2

Caller Cards

6	10	25
20	0	20
15	8	70
10	9	30
16	40	30
21	90	15
20	27	50
24	14	40

Maths KS1 Master File © EJP and DCP

Tens and units

This is a tower of ten cubes.   These are unit cubes.

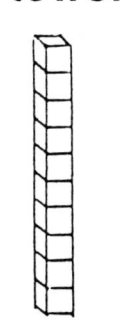

Draw two towers of ten cubes and four unit cubes.
What number is this?

Draw three towers of ten cubes and five unit cubes.
What number is this?

24 = ___tens + ___units.   35 = ___tens + ___units.

Now try these.

13 = ___ ten + ___ units

27 = ___ tens + ___units

36 = ___ tens + ___units

40 = ___ tens + ___units

57 = ___ tens + ___units

60 = ___ tens + ___units

61 = ___ tens + ___ unit

77 = ___ tens + ___units

87 = ___ tens + ___units

90 = ___ tens + ___units

Matching numbers

Here are lockers, keys and luggage. Colour those with the same numbers in the same colour. Begin by colouring locker 25, key twenty five and case 2 tens + 5 in red.

11	12	13	14	15	16	17	18	19	20
21	22	23	24	25	26	27	28	29	30
31	32	33	34	35	36	37	38	39	40

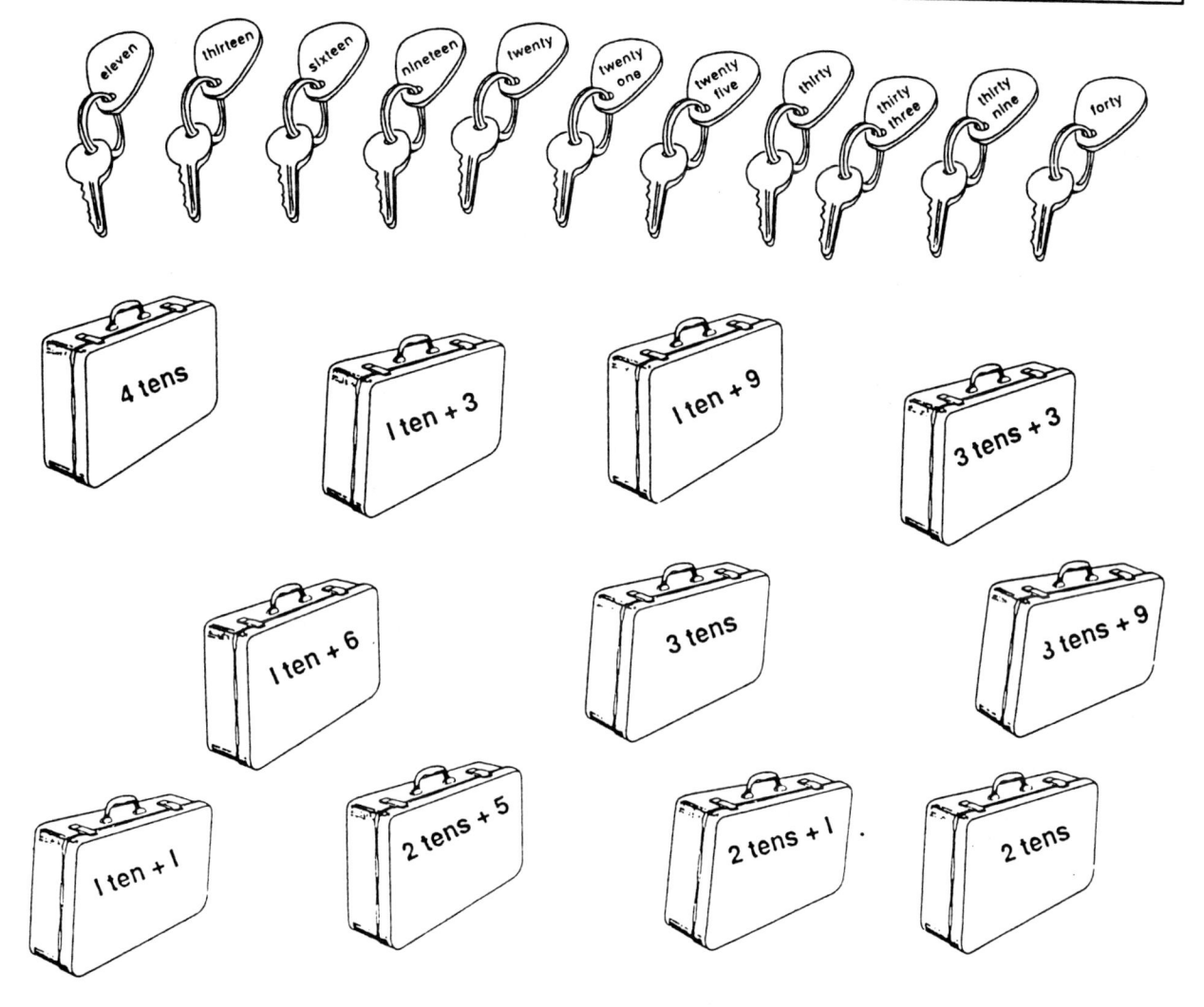

Keys: eleven, thirteen, sixteen, nineteen, twenty, twenty one, twenty five, thirty, thirty three, thirty nine, forty

Luggage: 4 tens, 1 ten + 3, 1 ten + 9, 3 tens + 3, 1 ten + 6, 3 tens, 3 tens + 9, 1 ten + 1, 2 tens + 5, 2 tens + 1, 2 tens

Maths KS1 Master File © EJP and DCP

Number Level 3 Matching Numbers 55

Bingo (addition/subtraction)

Paste the bingo and caller cards on to cardboard and cut out. Mix the caller cards and place in a pile face down. Choose a caller. The caller turns over the cards one at a time and calls out the numbers. The children cover the numbers on their bingo cards which have the same answer as the number called. For example, if 3 is called then 1 + 2 and 8-5 are covered. The winner is the one who covers his or her bingo card first. The class can make their own bingo cards.

5 + 2	6 - 2	1 + 1
4 - 3	4 + 1	5 - 3

5 - 2	6 + 2	10 - 1
9 + 1	7 - 1	5 + 3

1 + 2	10 - 3	3 + 7
5 - 3	3 + 0	9 - 3

9 - 6	3 + 3	8 - 7
3 - 0	8 - 4	9 + 1

Caller Cards

2	7	4
1	5	2

8	3	9
8	6	10

10	3	7
3	6	2

3	10	4
1	3	6

Sums to 20

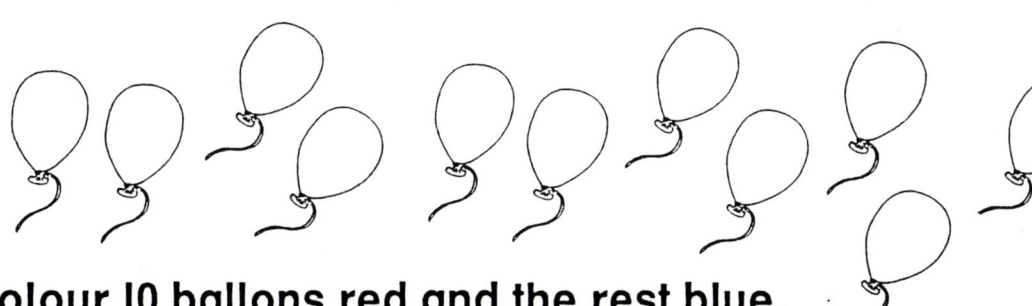

Colour 10 ballons red and the rest blue.
How many altogether? ☐

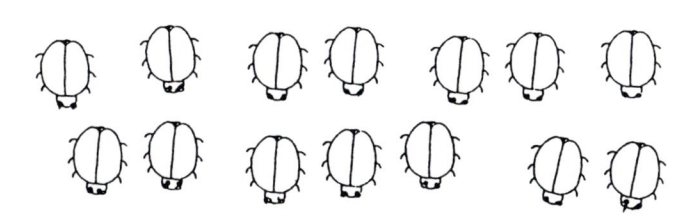

12 = 10 + ☐

Colour 10 beetles red and the rest green.
How many altogether? ☐

14 = 10 + ☐

Colour 10 mushrooms red and the rest yellow.
How many altogether? ☐

16 = 10 + ☐

Find the missing numbers

13 = 10 + ☐   15 = 10 + ☐

☐ = 10 + 2   ☐ = 10 + 9

Sums to 20

Colour the strawberries red. ☐
How many altogether? ☐
If 2 are eaten, how many are left? ☐

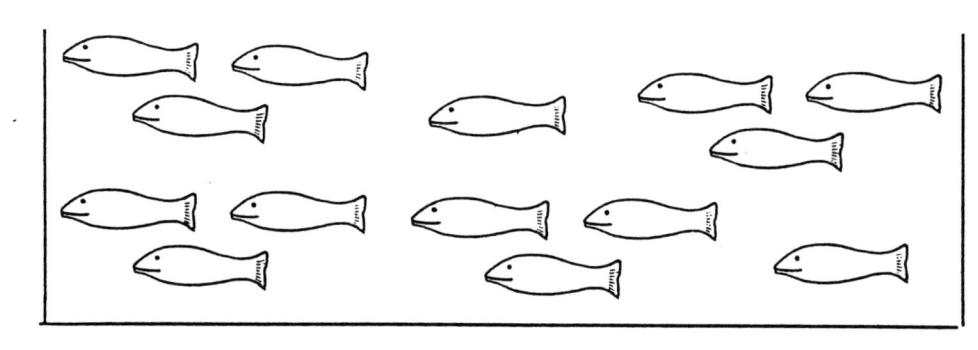

Colour 3 fish green, 5 blue and 6 red. ☐
How many altogether?
If 7 are taken out of the tank, how many fish are left? ☐

Find the numbers

13 - 3 = ☐   16 - 2 = ☐

17 - 5 = ☐   19 - 10 = ☐

18 - 5 = ☐   20 - 8 = ☐

12 - ☐ = 10   16 - ☐ = 12

18 - ☐ = 15   ☐ - 3 = 14

Numbers to 1000

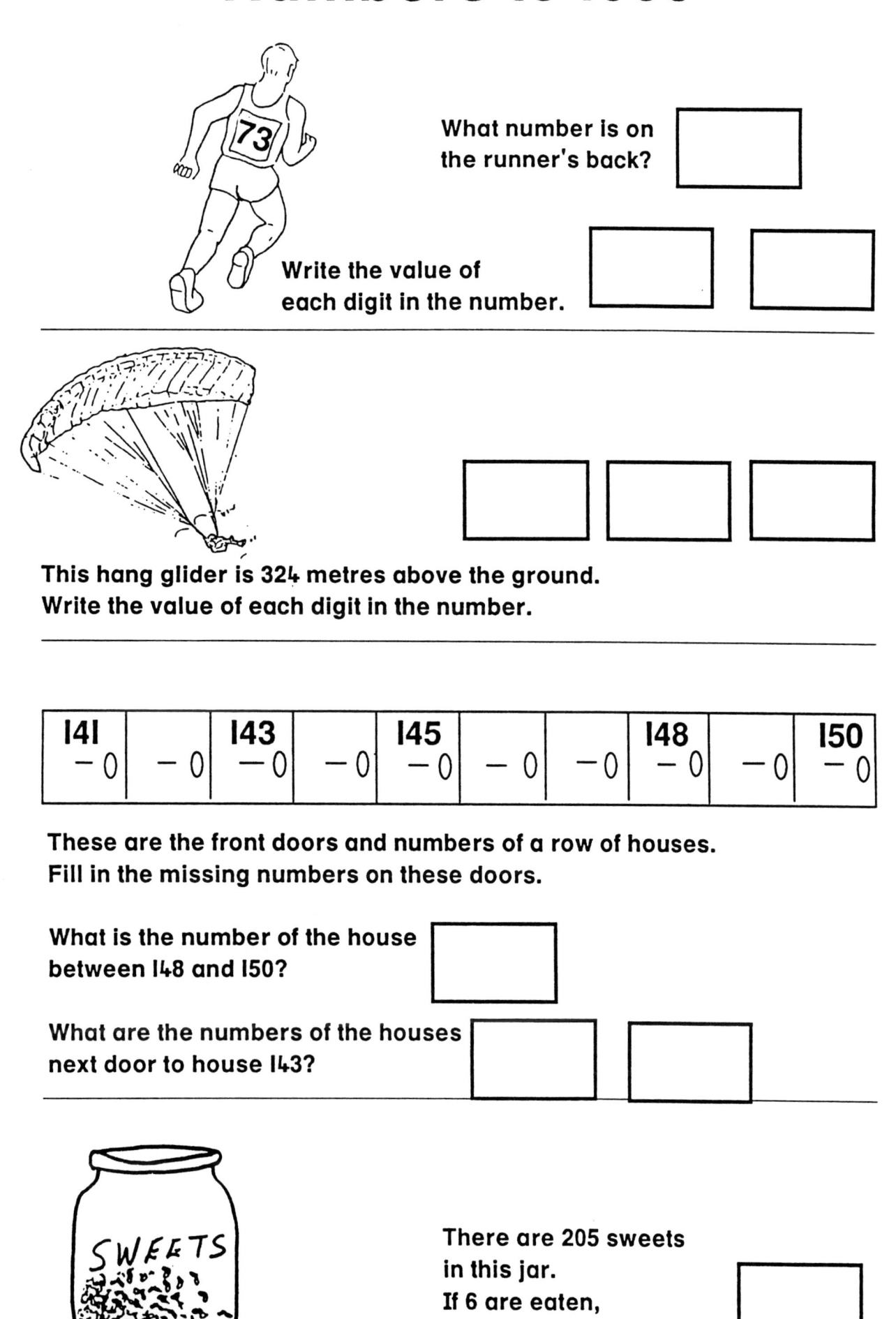

What number is on the runner's back? ☐

Write the value of each digit in the number. ☐ ☐

☐ ☐ ☐

This hang glider is 324 metres above the ground.
Write the value of each digit in the number.

141		143		145			148		150

These are the front doors and numbers of a row of houses.
Fill in the missing numbers on these doors.

What is the number of the house between 148 and 150? ☐

What are the numbers of the houses next door to house 143? ☐ ☐

There are 205 sweets in this jar.
If 6 are eaten, how many are left? ☐

Numbers to 1000

Look at these numbers. Put them in order beginning with the smallest and ending with the biggest. Then answer the questions below.

23, 5, 467, 734, 342, 78

_____

Which number has 3 in the units place? _____

Which number has 7 in the tens place? _____

Which number has 4 in the hundreds place?
_____

Which number is smaller than 10? _____

_____

A number has 6 in the units place, 3 in the tens place and 8 in the hundreds place. What is the number?

_____

10 more than 25 is _____   4 more than 68 is _____

3 less than 57 is _____   5 more than 197 is _____

The number between 68 and 70 is _____

The number bigger than 998 and smaller than 1000 is

_____

Numbers in words

Join the numbers with the same value.

26   108
one hundred and eight
two thousand, four hundred and thirty eight   761   four
2438   twenty six   seven hundred and sixty one

Write the numbers in words or figures.

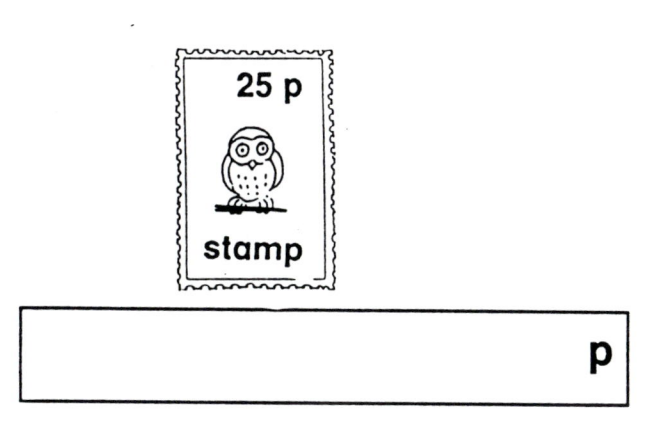

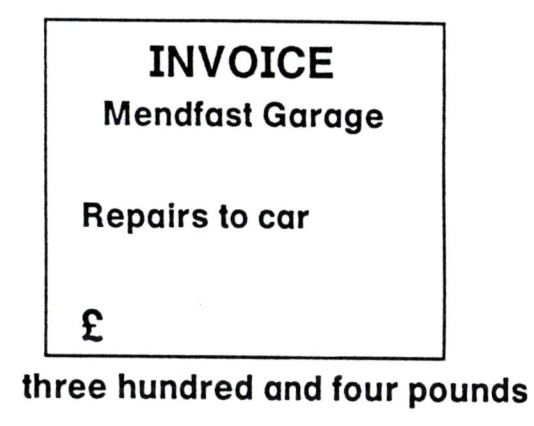

25 p stamp

_____ p

INVOICE
Mendfast Garage

Repairs to car

£

three hundred and four pounds

RECEIPT
Quicksilver Electricals
Received with thanks

£15

_____ pounds

POSTAL ORDER

Pay _____

£ _____

twenty five pounds.

Holiday Savings Bank   _____

Pay _____
Nine thousand, four hundred and ten pounds.

£ _____

Division

24 cakes are shared between the children at a party. How many does each have?

- 4 children → ☐ each
- 3 children → ☐ each
- 6 children → ☐ each
- 8 children → ☐ each
- 12 children → ☐ each

30 pieces of cheese are shared between the mice. How many pieces does each mouse get?

- 2 mice → ☐ each
- 3 mice → ☐ each
- 5 mice → ☐ each
- 6 mice → ☐ each
- 10 mice → ☐ each
- 15 mice → ☐ each

The school buses each carry 20 people. How many buses will be needed to carry 54 children and 3 teachers? _____

15   23   100   60   32   5   48   40   10   75

Draw a ring around each number that can be divided by 10 without any remainder.

Draw a square around each number that can be divided by 5 without any remainder.

Write three other numbers that can be divided by 5 and 10 without any remainders.

☐   ☐   ☐

Multiplication

A woman buys 5 boxes of eggs costing £1.20 a box. How much does she pay?

If there are 6 eggs in each box, how many eggs does she buy?

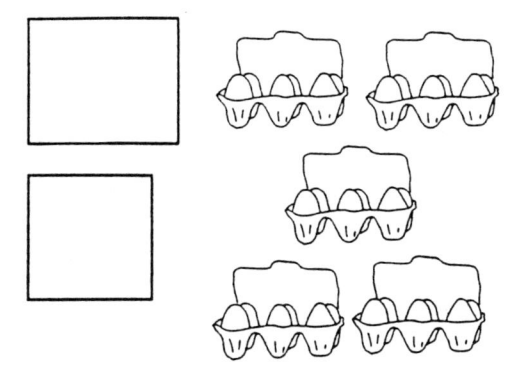

John eats twice as many sweets as Jane. If Jane eats 3 sweets, how many does John eat?

Each morning, William earns £2 for delivering newspapers. He does not deliver them on Sundays. How much does he earn in a week?

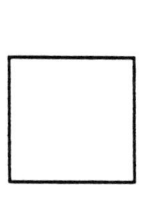

Work out the total cost of this shopping.

1 jar of coffee	@ £1.25	= £1.25
3 oranges	@ 30p each	=
5 ices	@ 15p each	=
2 loaves of bread	@ 35p each	=
4 cakes	@ 20p each	=
	Total	£

Work out these sums as fast as you can.

5 X 2 = ____   8 X 5 = ____   1 X 5 = ____

2 X 6 = ____   10 X 6 = ____   7 X 2 = ____

3 X 5 = ____   7 X 5 = ____   6 X 5 = ____

9 X 3 = ____   10 X 10 = ____   9 X 2 = ____

Units

What is the length of Slinky Sylvia in centimetres ☐ millimetres? ☐

Put a tick in the correct boxes.

Would you measure the playground in

millimetres ☐   centimetres ☐   metres ☐   kilometres ☐ ?

Would this runner weigh himself in

grams ☐   kilograms ☐   tonnes ☐ ?

How much milk would he drink in a day?

1 millilitre ☐   half a litre ☐ ?

Fill in the units.

There are 24 _____ in a day.

There are 7 _____ in a week.

There are 4 _____ in a month.

There are 12 _____ in a year.

The age of a baby (less than a year old) is measured in _____

and _____

Your age is measured in _____ and _____

Measuring

Measure these distances in centimetres.

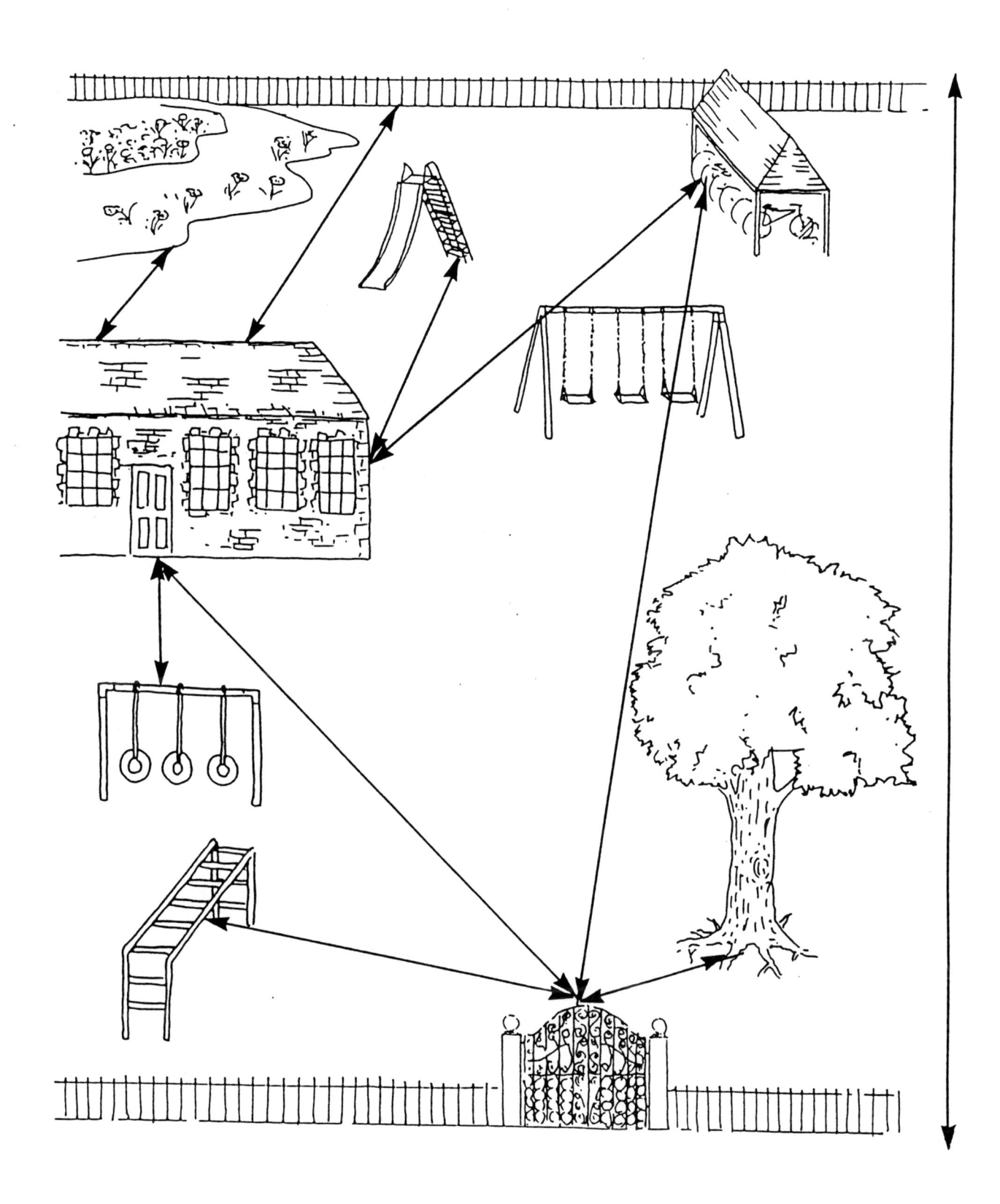

Make a drawing like this of your school.
Measure the distances in strides and metres.

Money

You buy a key-ring for 21p.
How much change from 50p?

85p £2.25 £1.50
20p 26p

These clothes were bought at a car boot sale. How much did they cost?

How many of these bars of chocolate can you buy for £1?

BIG THE BAR 26p

How much change is there?

You buy these in a newsagents. How much do they cost altogether?

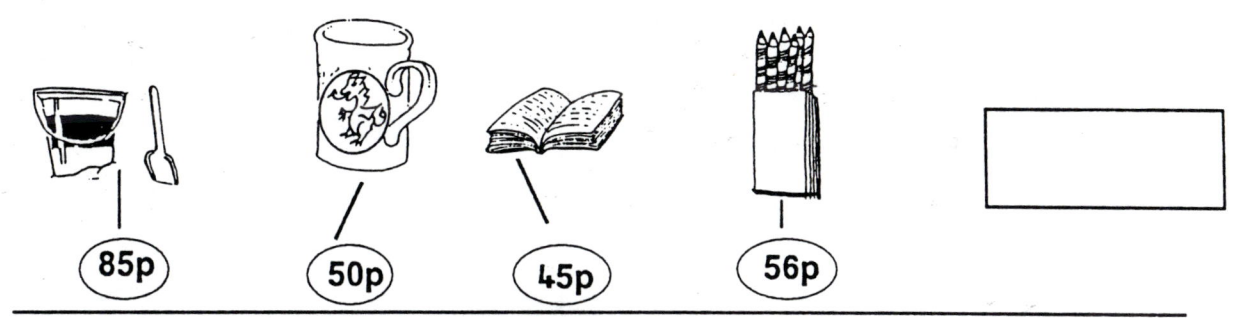

85p   50p   45p   56p

You have £2 to buy two presents.
Draw circles around the ones you buy.

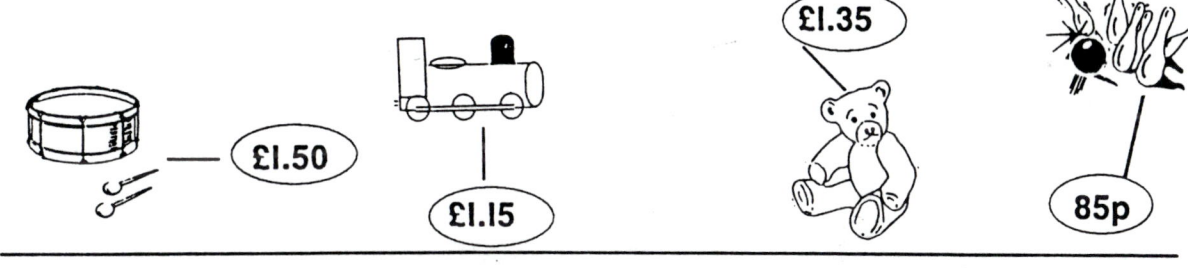

£1.50   £1.15   £1.35   85p

You and four friends go to the cinema. The tickets are £1.50 each and you each have an ice cream costing 26p each. How much change do you have from £10?

Silver Screen Cinema £1.50

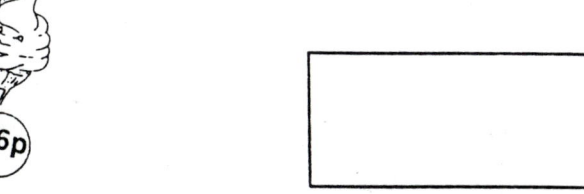

26p

Time

Write the time for each of these clocks.

Draw these times on the clocks.

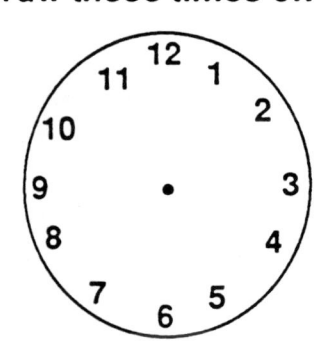

5 o'clock   half past four   quarter to two

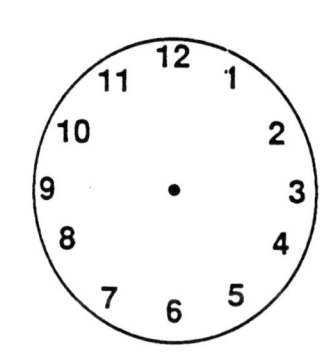

What time do you go to bed? _____

What time does your favourite TV programme start? _____

What time does your favourite TV programme end? _____

How long is this programme? _____

More time

Put in the hands.

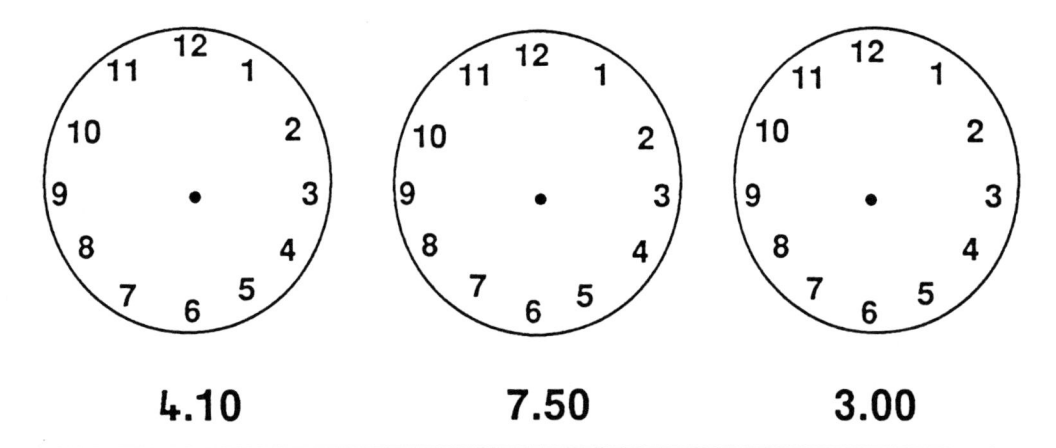

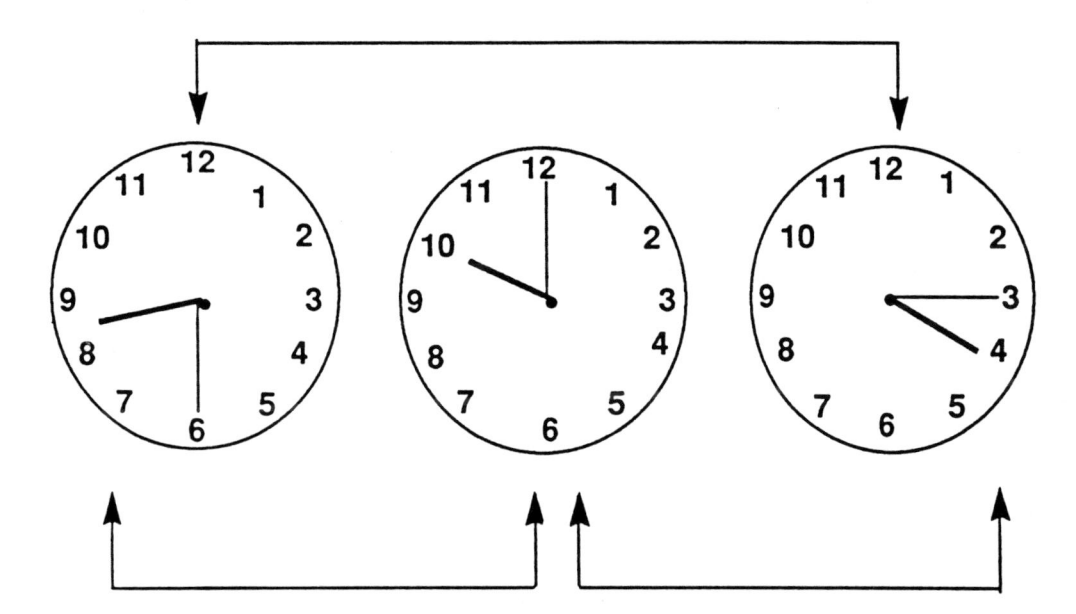

```
   4.10            7.50            3.00
```

What is the difference in time between these clocks?

Write the digital times in the watch faces.

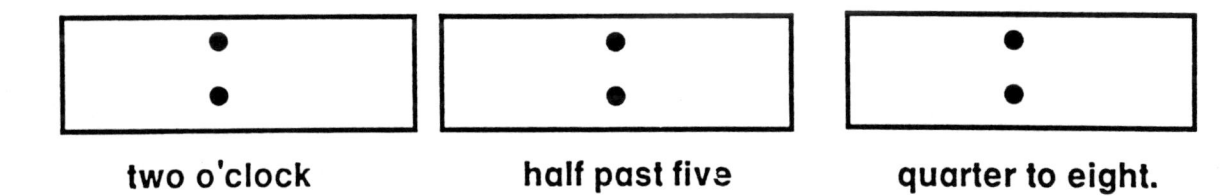

two o'clock   half past five   quarter to eight.

Write these times in words.

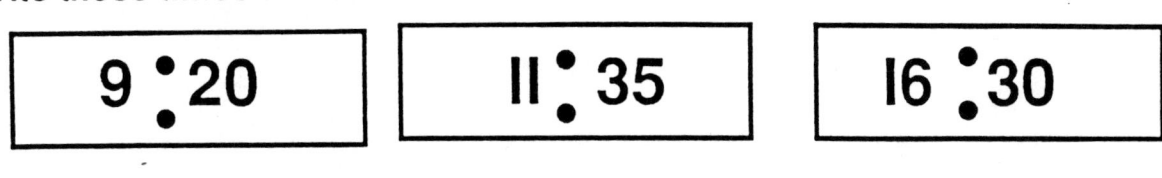

9:20   11:35   16:30

_____   _____   _____

Negative numbers

This is a lift in a large store. Ground floor is 0 and the floor numbers are like a number line. Use the floor numbers to answer these questions.

Start at 0 and go up 3 floors.
Which floor number are you on now?

What number is 3 more than 0?

Start at 5 and go down 4 floors.
Which floor number are you on now?

What number is 4 less than 5?

Start at 0 and go down 2 floors.
Which floor number are you on now?

What number is 2 less than 0?

Start at -3 and go up 3 floors.
Which floor number are you on now?

What number is 3 bigger than -3?

Start at 1 and go down 4 floors.
Which floor number are you on now?

What number is 4 less than 1?

What is the temperature on this thermometer?

If the temperature falls by 15°, what will the temperature be?

If the temperature on the thermometer rises by 5°, what will the temperature be?

Lift floors:
- Roof Garden — 5
- Offices — 4
- Restaurant — 3
- Furniture — 2
- Leisure Wear — 1
- Fashion — 0 Ground
- Toy Fayre — -1
- Santa's Grotto — -2
- Electrical Dept — -3
- Car Park — -4
- Bus Station — -5

Lists

Make a list of ten friends. Put them in 2 columns

Girls   Boys

Make a list of 6 things you like to eat. Begin with your favourite food.

Make two lists from these objects using the headings toy shop and pet shop.

Look at this shopping list.
butter
milk
sugar
coffee
tea

If you were sent to the supermarket with this list, what more information would you need?

Make a shopping list for the supermarket for your family.

Linking

Draw a tail on each mouse.

Draw lines to show what goes into the duffle bag and what goes into the lunch box.

Today John is 3 years old, David is 6 years old, Jane is 5 and Mary is 4. Write their names under these birthday cakes.

_____   _____   _____   _____

This drawing shows how many pets Kevin and his friends have.

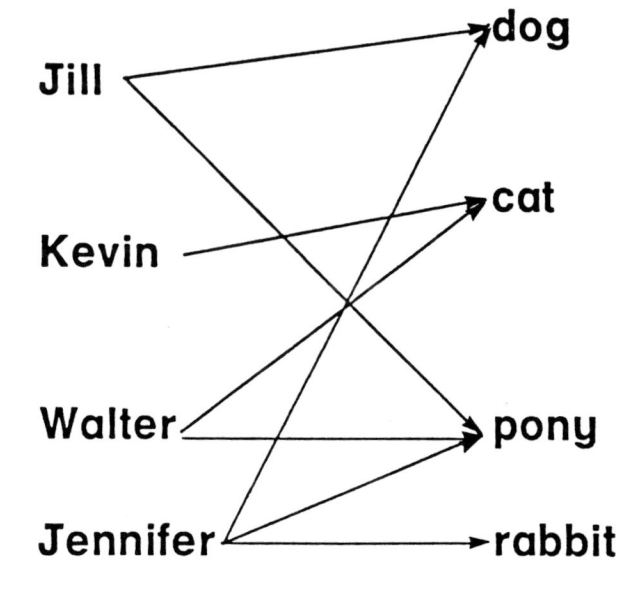

What pets does Jill have?
_____

Who has a pony and a cat?
_____

What pet does Kevin have?
_____

Who has the most pets?
_____

Who has a pony?
_____

Draw a diagram like this to show how many pets your friends have.

Count and record

Count the objects and write the numbers in the boxes.

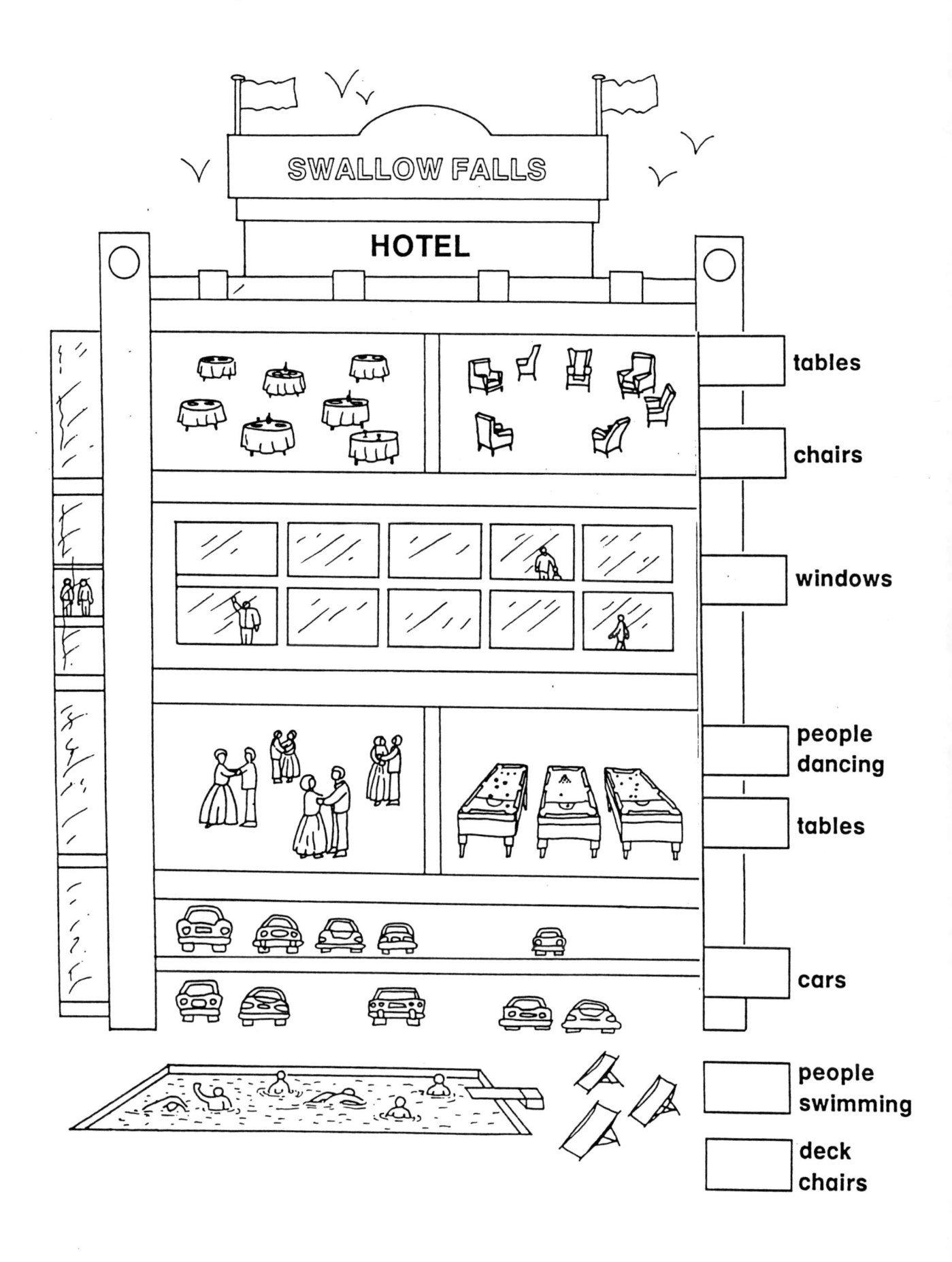

SWALLOW FALLS
HOTEL

- tables
- chairs
- windows
- people dancing
- tables
- cars
- people swimming
- deck chairs

Maths KS1 Master File © EJP and DCP

Picture graphs

These are the favourite ice lollies of a group of children.

Orange	🍦 🍦 🍦 🍦 🍦 🍦
Strawberry	🍦 🍦 🍦
Chocolate	🍭 🍭 🍭 🍭 🍭
Rockets	🚀 🚀 🚀 🚀 🚀 🚀 🚀 🚀

Which lolly is liked best? _____

Which lolly is liked least? _____

Which lollies are equally popular? _____

How many children were asked? _____

_____

12 children were asked which fruit they liked best. 6 said they liked apples best, 4 said they liked bananas and 2 said they liked pears best. Draw small pictures of the fruit in the graph below to show these answers.

	Number of fruits
apples	🍎
bananas	🍌
pears	🍐

Picture graphs

This picture graph shows how many vehicles pass the school in ten minutes.

Cars   Buses   Lorries

How many cars passed the school? _____

How many lorries passed the school? _____

How many vehicles passed the school altogether? _____

Use this form to find out how 10 of your friends travelled to school.

Name _____   Age _____   Class _____

How did you travel to school last week? Please tick one box.
by car ☐   by bus ☐   by bike ☐   by walking ☐

Draw figures like this 👤 to show the results on this graph.

by car   by bus   by bike   by walking

Waiting for the bus

Waiting for the bus.

This frequency chart shows how many people are waiting for a bus at different times.

	8 am	11.30 am	4 pm
Mon.	////	///	////
Tues.	///	////	//////
Wed.	/////	///	//
Thurs.	///	//	////
Fri.	/	//	///

How many people were at the bus stop on Tuesday at 8 am? _____

How many people caught the bus on Wednesday? _____

On what day did most people catch the bus? _____

How many people travelled on the bus throughout the week? _____

Find out how many children travel on your school bus each day in a week.

Use this information to make a frequency chart for your school.

Bar graphs

This bar graph shows how many children in a class have blonde, brown, black or ginger hair.

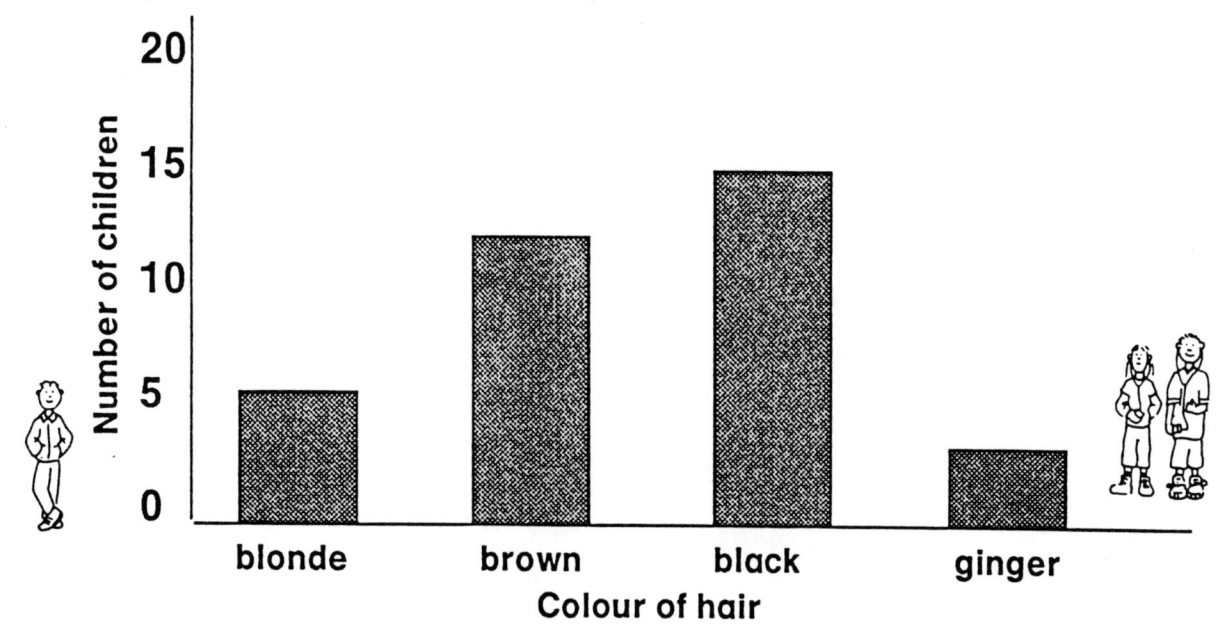

How many children have brown hair? _____

How many children have ginger hair? _____

How many children are in the class? _____

Draw a bar graph like this for your class.

This graph shows the height of the children in a class.

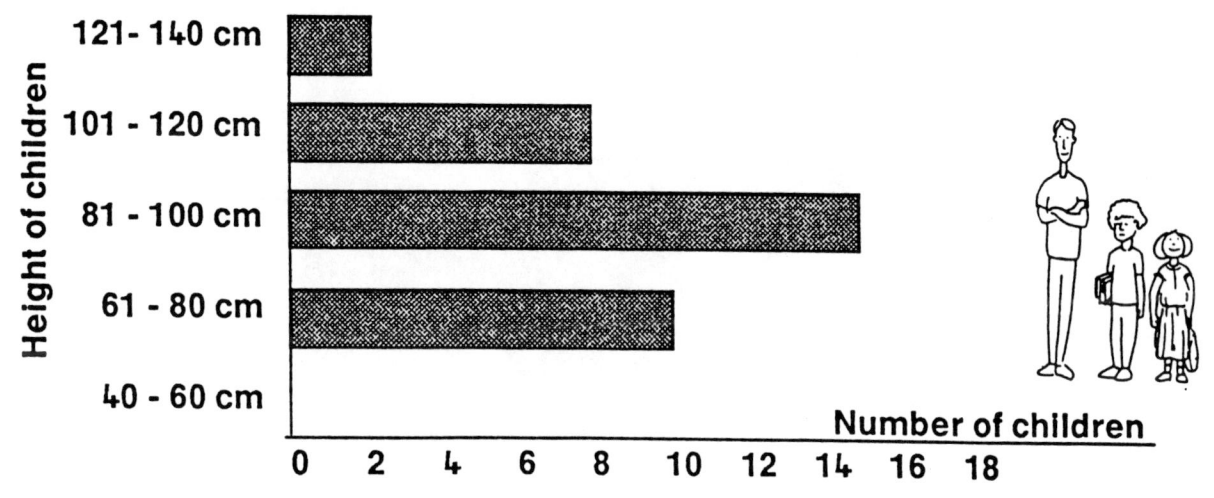

How many children are between 61 - 80 cm tall? _____

How many children are taller than 101 cm? _____

There are 3 children between 40 - 60 cm tall. Mark these on the graph.

How many children were measured altogether? _____

What is the weather like?

Mon.	Tues.	Wed.	Thurs.	Fri.	Sat.	Sun.
	1 ☀	2 ☀	3 ☁	4 🌧	5 ☁	6 ☀
7 ☀	8 ☁	9 ☁	10 🌧	11 ☀	12 ☀	13 ☀
14 ☀	15 ☁	16 ☁	17 🌧	18 ☁	19 ☁	20 ☀
21 ☀	22 ☀	23 ☁	24 🌧	25 ☁	26 ☀	27 ☀
28 ☁	29 🌧	30 🌧	31 ☁			

sunny ☀   cloudy ☁   rainy 🌧

This is a weather chart for a month.
Colour it then put the information on the weather chart in this frequency table.

sunny days	
cloudy days	
rainy days	

On how many days did it rain? _____
On how many days did the sun shine? _____
How many days were cloudy? _____

Sorting and recording

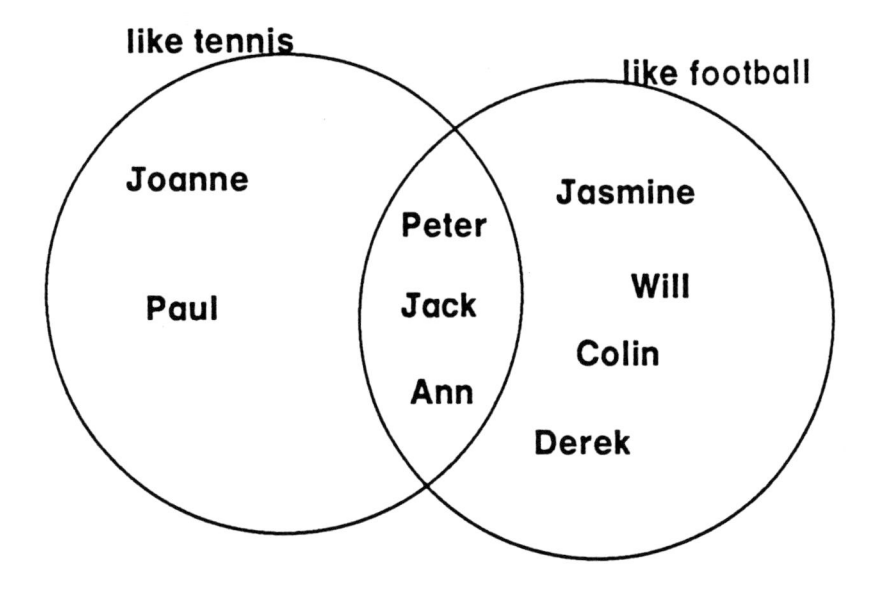

like tennis — like football

- Joanne
- Paul
- Peter
- Jack
- Ann
- Jasmine
- Will
- Colin
- Derek

Name the pupils who like tennis but not football. _____

How many pupils like football but not tennis? _____

How many pupils like football and tennis? _____

_____

The number of pupils in a class who can or cannot swim is recorded in this Carroll diagram.

	girls	boys
can swim	12	11
cannot swim	4	3

How many boys cannot swim? _____   How many boys can swim? _____

How many girls cannot swim? _____   How many girls can swim? _____

How many students are in the class? _____

Where is it?

Look at the picture and draw rings around the correct words.

The birds are flying in/by the sky.

The owl is perched over/on the branch.

The farmer is behind/beside the tractor.

The dog is on/under the tree.

The frightened cat is climbing up/down the tree.

The boy is near/on the fence.

The ivy is growing around/away from the fence.

The rabbit is outside/inside the hutch.

Draw three apples in the tree.

Draw a rabbit in front of the tractor.

Draw a cloud above the birds.

Draw a mouse at the bottom of the tree.

How many legs does the cat have? _____

How many legs on the dog can you see? _____

How many legs does the dog have? _____

How many wheels are on the tractor? _____

Now colour the picture.

Maths KS1 Master File © EJP and DCP   Shape and Space Level 1 Position

Measuring words

Draw rings around the objects.

The tallest alien.

The bug with the most spots.

The fattest man.

The youngest elephant.

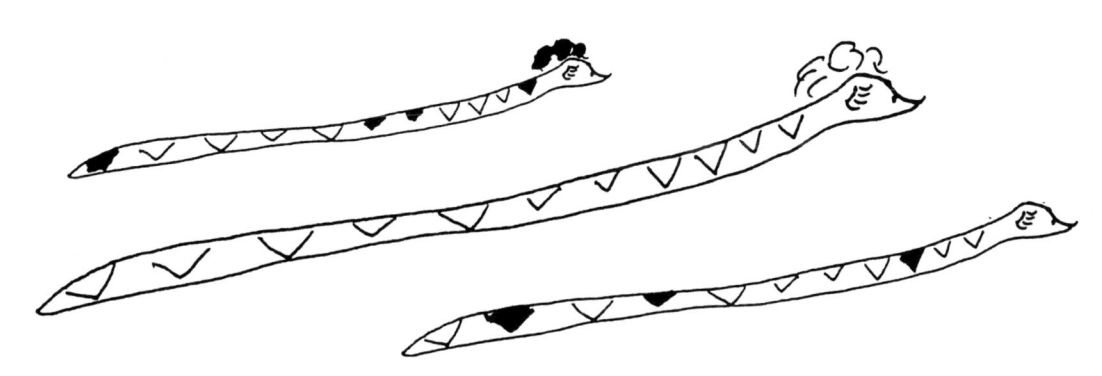

The longest snake.

This is the Mouse family.

Maximillian    Minnie    Midge

Which is the smallest mouse? _____
Which is bigger than Minnie? _____

2-D shapes

Colour the squares red, the rectangles green, the triangles yellow and the circles green.

These shapes are swimming in a pool.
Draw the whole shape of each one.

3-D shapes

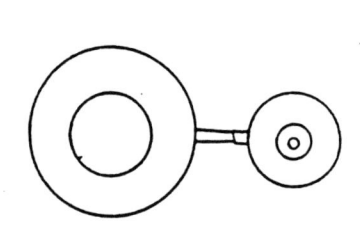

Can you guess what this is?

A woman wearing a big hat frying an egg in a pan.

Join each shape to its name.

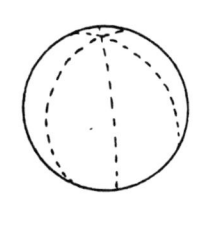

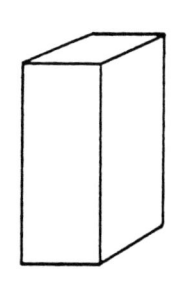

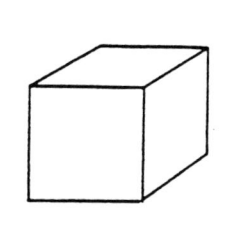

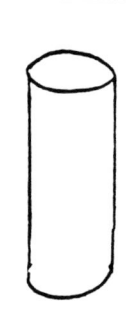

cube   sphere   cylinder   cuboid

These are unusual views of some objects. Link these views with the objects.

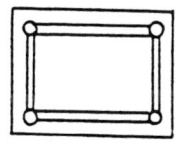

**These are the tops of some 3-D shapes.
Join each top to the correct shape.**

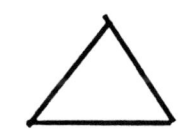

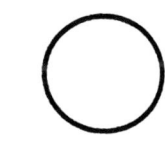

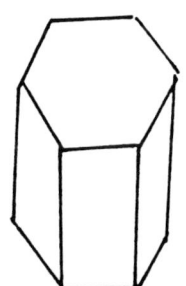

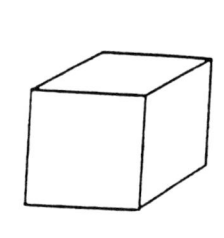

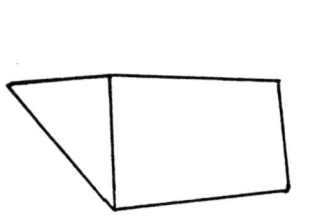

Imagine you are in a hot air balloon flying over your school. What would the tops of the buildings look like?

Shape and Space Level 2 3-D Shapes

Matching shapes and sides

Match the names, sides and shapes.

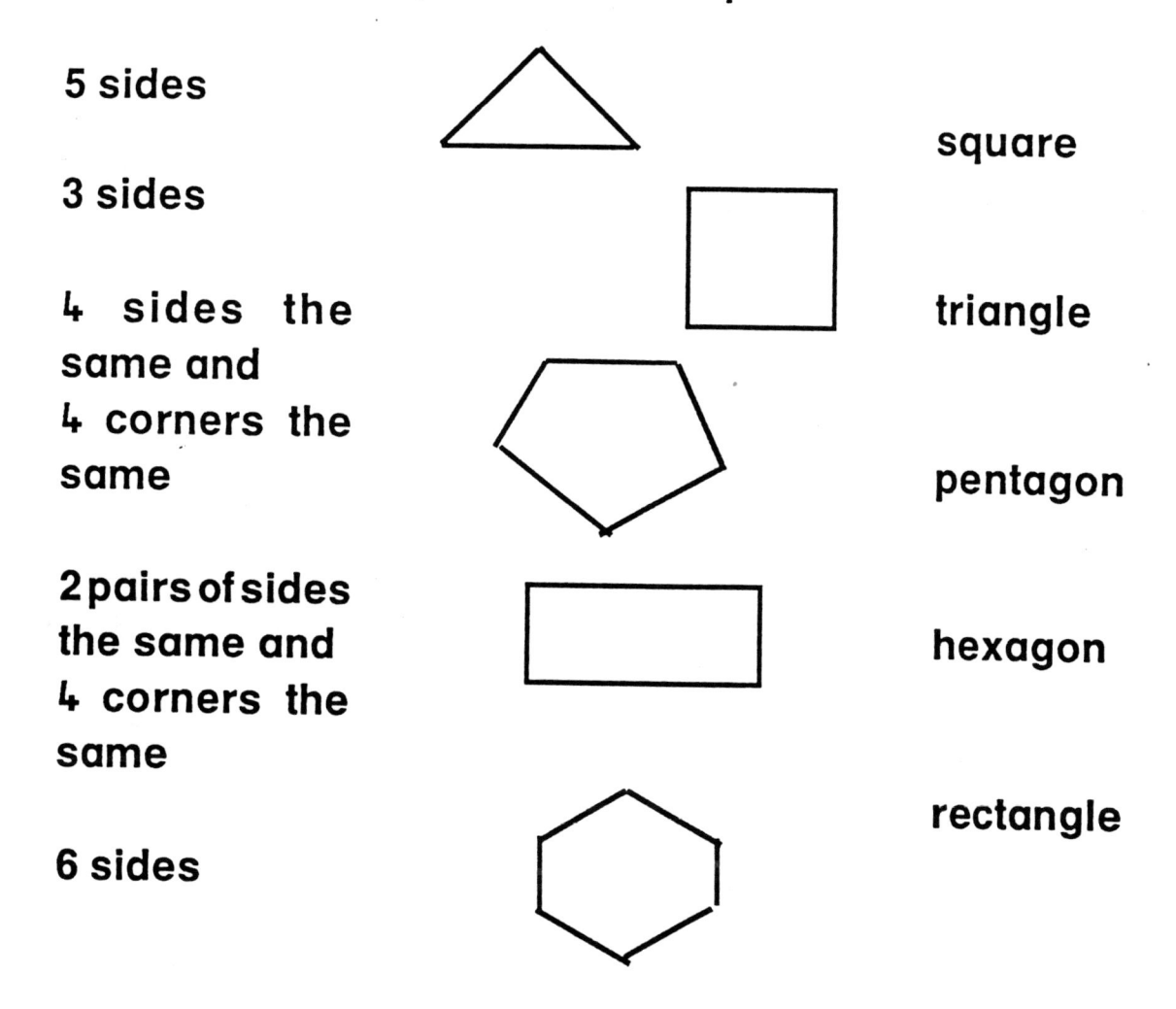

5 sides

3 sides

4 sides the same and
4 corners the same

2 pairs of sides the same and
4 corners the same

6 sides

square

triangle

pentagon

hexagon

rectangle

In these drawings, colour the squares yellow, rectangles blue, triangles green and circles pink.

Angles

Here are some right angles.

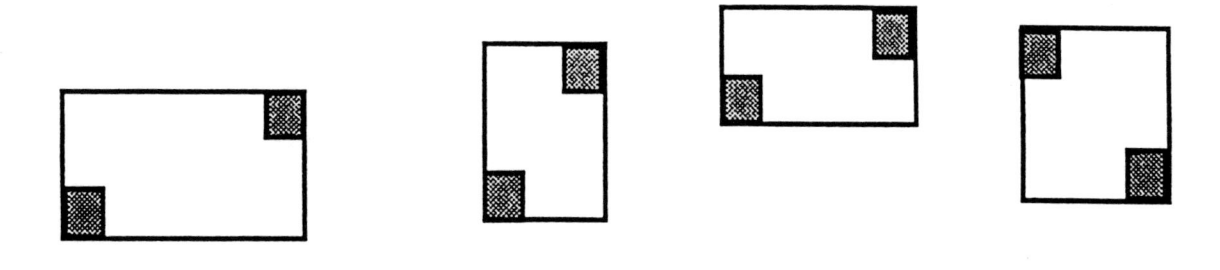

Look for right angles all around you. Draw what you see. Here are some clues to help you start. Look at

the door

a book

the window

a pencil box

your table or desk

the corners of the room

Look at the angles below. Colour the right angles red.
Colour green the angles which are bigger than a right angle.
Colour blue the angles which are smaller than a right angle.

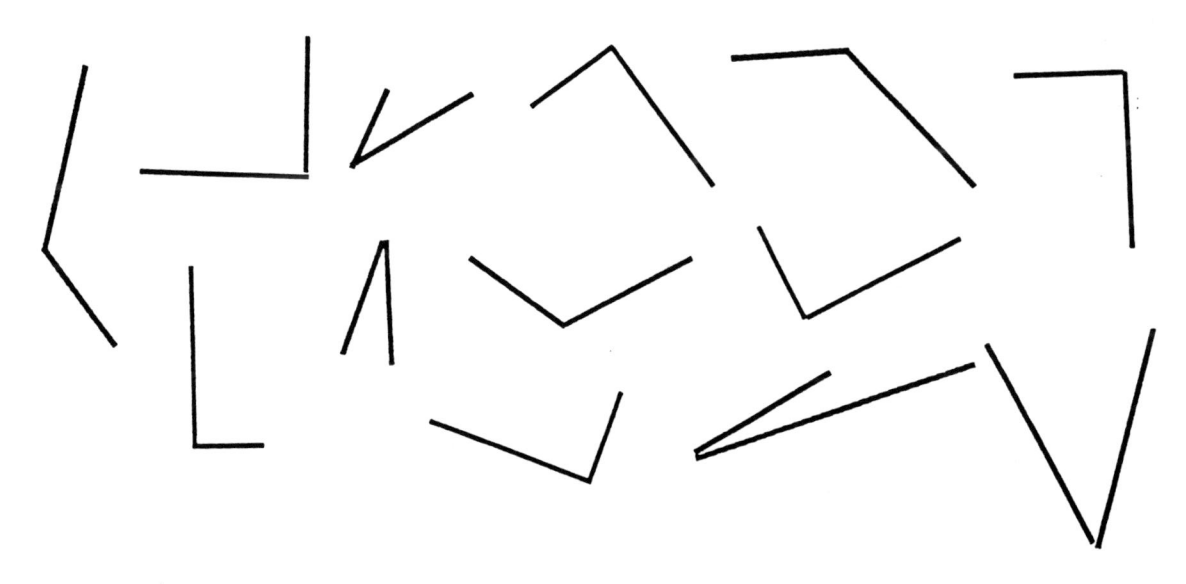

What kinds of angles can your elbow make?

Moving

Draw a ring around the words which show which way the envelopes are moved.

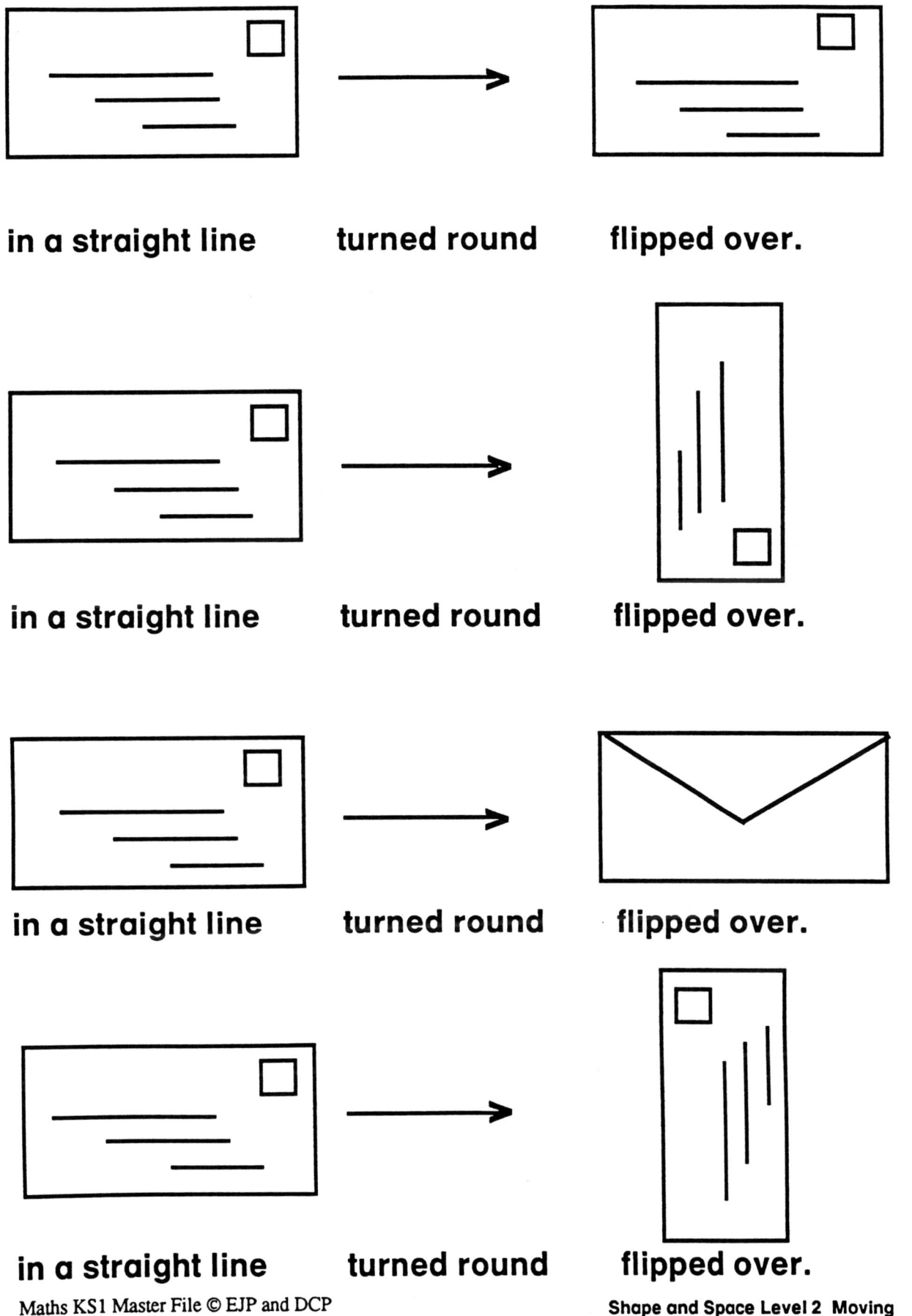

in a straight line   turned round   flipped over.

in a straight line   **turned round**   flipped over.

in a straight line   turned round   **flipped over.**

in a straight line   **turned round**   **flipped over.**

Symmetrical shapes

**Half of these shapes have been drawn.
Draw the other halves to make symmetrical shapes.**

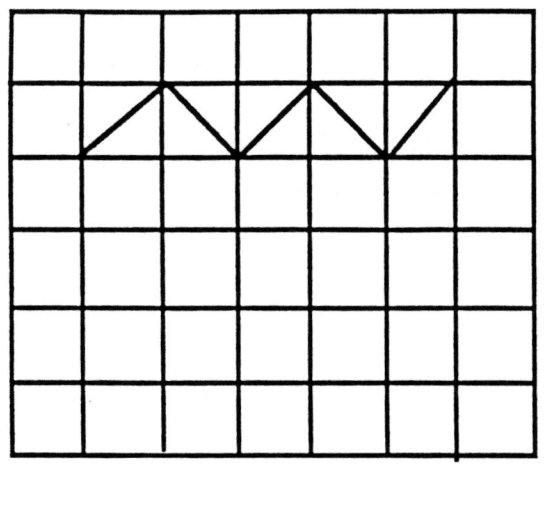

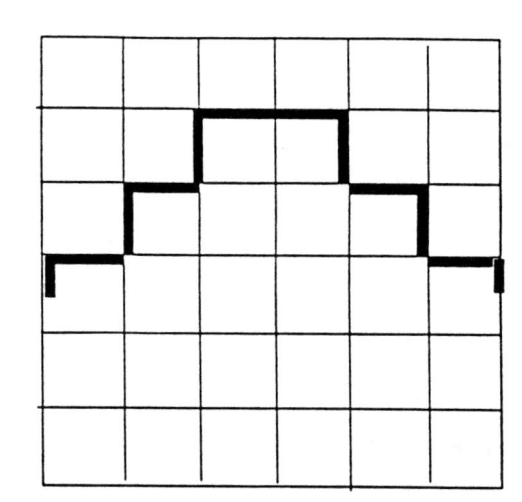

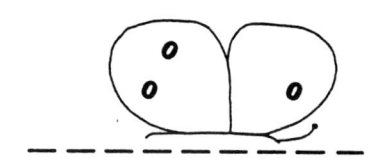

Colour all the symmetrical drawings and letters.

A B H K M

O T U X Y

Are there any symmetrical letters in your name?

Find the treasure

This is a map of an island where treasure is buried. The letters show which column a landmark is in and numbers show which row the landmark is in. There are sharks in A5. Colour the map and find the other landmarks.

Olli Octopus is in _____

The pirates weighed anchor in _____

Jake posed for his photograph in _____

There is a secret map in _____

There is a skull and crossbones in _____

There is the head of a monster in _____

There is a lake in _____

The pirates camped in _____

Where is there a volcano? _____

Where are there flying fish? _____

Where is the treasure? _____

Draw a forest in B3.

Draw a giant spider in D4.

Draw a slithery snake in C3.

Draw a toad in A2.

Write a secret message in D5.

Maths KS1 Master File © EJP and DCP   Shape and Space Level 3 Co-ordinates   87

Points of the compass

Mark the points of the compass

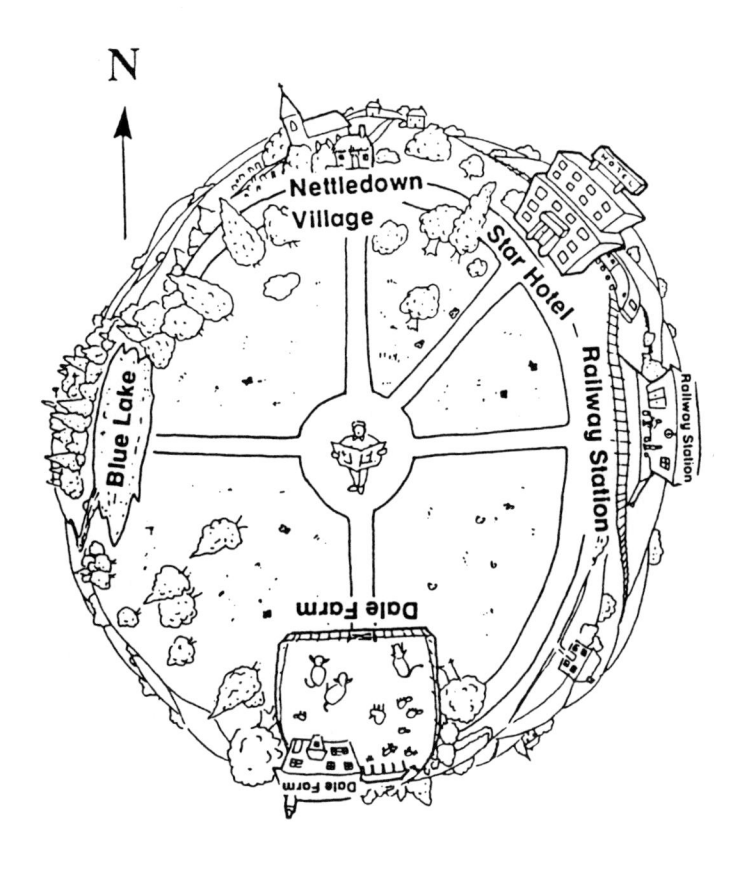

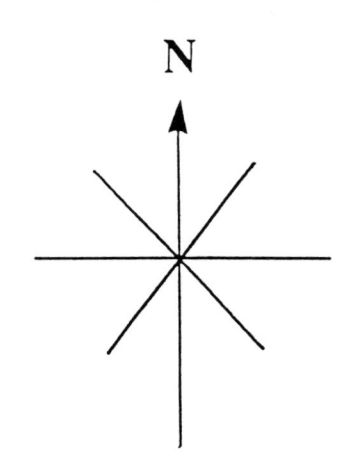

Which way should the walker go

to reach the hotel? _____

to reach the lake? _____

to reach the village? _____

to reach the farm? _____

to reach the railway station? _____

Follow the clues to reach the treasure.

Maths KS1 Master File © EJP and DCP   Shape and Space Level 3 Points of the Compass 88

Clockwise or anticlockwise?

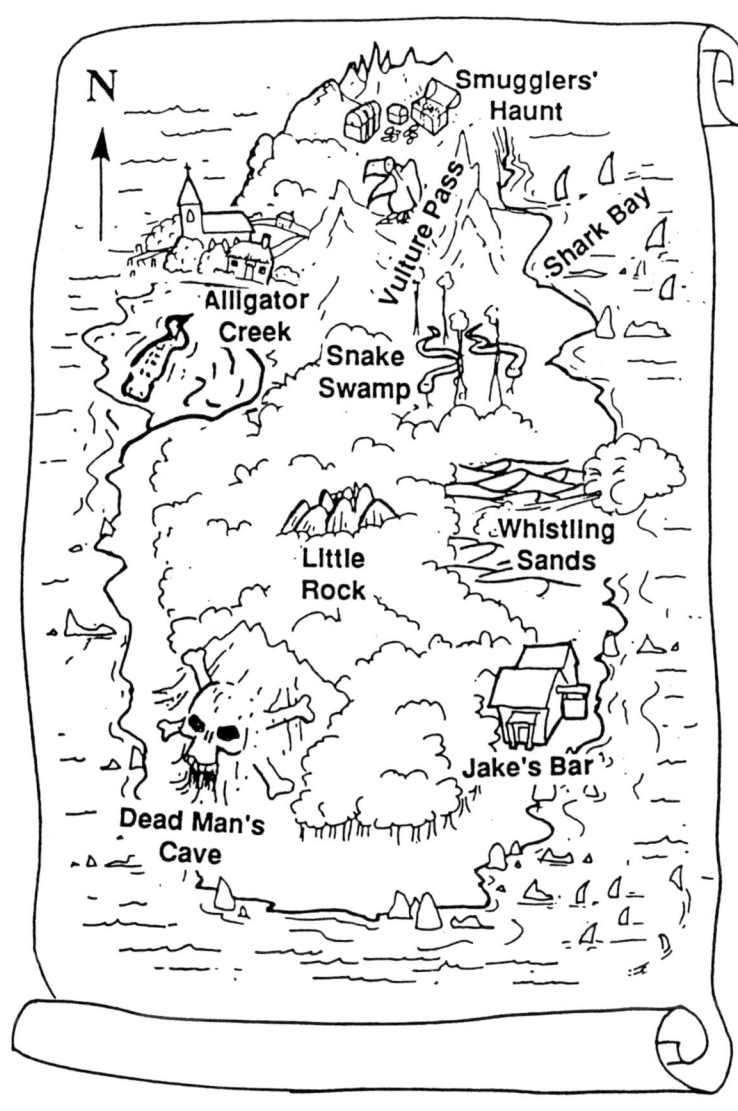

Clockwise or anticlockwise?

If you walk along the path from the village of Alligator Creek to Smugglers' Haunt, you are walking in a clockwise or anticlockwise direction?

_____

If you walk from Alligator Creek to Jake's Bar in an anticlockwise direction you pass

_____

If you walk from Smugglers' Haunt to Whistling Sands in a clockwise direction you pass

_____

Find the buried treasure.

Follow these directions. Mark your route on the map and put X where the treasure is buried.

From Alligator Creek walk south east to Jake's Bar for food and drink.

Then travel north along the coast road making your way carefully through Whistling Sands, around Shark Bay to meet Pete at Smugglers' Haunt.

Then go south through Vulture Pass and then west working your way quietly around Snake Swamp. Continue to Little Rock.

From Little Rock, travel south west to Dead Man's Cave.

Continue along the coast road to the most southern tip of the island where you will find the treasure.

_____

Tell a friend about the route you follow from your home to school.
Draw a map of the route.
Include a compass and the names of some of the buildings and streets.

TEACHERS' NOTES AND RESOURCES

The very early teaching of mathematics is the most important part of a child's development in the subject: at this time, a child can learn to enjoy it and find it fun. Attitudes developed here are likely to stay with the child for a long time - sometimes for life. Above all, teaching requires a love of the subject, imagination, patience and more patience. Those who find mathematics easy must realise that not everyone is so fortunate. All too often we hear 'I'm no good at maths. I hated the subject at school.' Mathematics is part of our daily lives: shopping, cooking, sewing, building, almost everything is measured and calculated. Time, cost, mass, the list is endless.

Fortunately, most of us are better at mathematics than we think. We juggle complicated facts and figures, make split second estimates and decisions and mostly do very well. We link litres/gallons of petrol, fuel consumption, miles and time for journeys, we cope with railway timetables and schedules, we understand codes like traffic lights, we calculate exchange rates for holidays, cope with decimalisation and a mix of metric and imperial units. Confusion and fear arise when this mass of material is unfamiliar.

When we meet a new situation we immediately apply our personal experience to deal with it. If necessary we experiment and extend information we have stored mentally until we can cope. Children, especially young ones, soak up information like blotting paper. Everything is a challenge and one of the joys of teaching is seeing children grow in confidence.

The early years of learning are the most important in the development of mathematical ability. It is at this stage that children become interested or bored, love the subject or hate it and above all become confident or confused and fearful of mathematical concepts. For example, failure to develop good spacial awareness may cause problems later in advanced disciplines such as engineering, craft, design and technology. Girls should be encouraged to play with teaching aids such as Lego just as the boys need to be encouraged to take part in cooking experiments.

It is important to begin teaching a new topic within the child's experience. Build on this and gradually extend it. Always start with material the child can handle confidently. If there are difficulties go back to earlier work and the security of familiar ground. Sometimes extra time for play is needed. Never allow a child to stay confused or worried.

Mathematics is best taught in context whenever possible. It should be practical. The drawing of a block of wood does not convey the reality of holding it in the hand, feeling the warmth, the texture and its hardness, looking at the colour or natural patterns of the grain, smelling the natural scents or paint. Young children learn best when things have a reality that they can touch, feel and hold.

Mathematics should be fun. There is much to talk about, new words to learn, experiments, games and puzzles to try. At all times link what is taught with experiences outside the classroom, in the 'real' world, with 'real' work.

Children love to see their work displayed. Sometimes it can go home to show to parents, who hopefully will appreciate its importance. As much as possible should be displayed in the classroom. It should be possible for everyone's work to be shown at some time. Displays should have clear headings so that everyone knows what they are about. Encourage children to draw pictures and later diagrams to illustrate their work.

Life is all about problem solving and so is mathematics. Children love to find solutions and have more satisfaction from their own results than from other people's. Problem solving also develops social skills, especially when they work in groups.

> Children have to learn to work together, co-operate with each other, to listen to the ideas of others and offer suggestions of their own.
>
> They have to develop strategies, experiment and try out ideas, test theories and modify them.
>
> They have to use skills learned and concepts acquired within the context of the problem to be solved. This helps to reinforce the usefulness of what they have learned.

NUMBER LEVELS 1 - 3

USING MATHS

This is about the ways in which children use maths carrying out everyday tasks in the classroom. It underpins much of the reason for teaching the subject and examines whether children understand and can apply what they have learned. For the purposes of assessment it is necessary to select suitable tasks such as counting crockery in the 'home corner' or putting the correct number of chairs around a table. This kind of assessment continues throughout the course in many different ways.

EARLY COUNTING

Children become familiar with numbers when they are very young. They know which toys and how many are theirs, what is their fair share of sweets or other goodies. Here, they are probably matching sets rather than counting or using numbers. Children quickly learn to sort familiar things such as different kinds of fruit or balloons. Here shape and colour form the basis of differentiation.

Use the information they have absorbed in their day to day lives. Most will be able to distinguish a puppy from its mother and one breed of dog from another. They will also have some idea of what they should wear to school.

These familiar things can be used to introduce the ideas of selection, comparison and sets.

Chanting, for example

1, 2, 3, 4, 5
Once I caught a fish alive
6, 7, 8, 9, 10
Then I let it go again

does not ensure that the child actually has any concept of what the numbers mean.

The teaching of number begins with things with which children are familiar - 1 hat, 1 coat, 1 desk, 1 chair, 2 shoes, 2 hands, 2 gloves, 2 eyes, 4 fingers and a thumb on each hand, and many teeth. Keep numbers small - the number of wheels on a bike, legs on a chair, buttons on a coat ... It is a good idea for the child to begin to write or trace numbers. The child will not understand the concept of '2' until he or she starts to associate the shape 2 with two sweets or two bricks and so on. Everyday associations are important such as how many pints of milk, how many newspapers or letters are delivered at home, how many children are absent from the class. Count piles of things with identical numbers. Remember to count from left to right from the children's point of view.

By children playing with things that can be counted at first to ten and then to a hundred, numbers become familiar and friendly. Children can make a list of the numbers that are important to them such as birthdays, the ages of brothers and sisters ... The number of the house or flat where a child lives is used as a name: 6, Orchard Lane would be just as identifiable as 'Rose Cottage', Orchard Lane.

Gradually children begin to associate each number with a different pile of items, to know that 3 is 'more' than 2, to begin to understand the concept of conservation of number.

It is important for children to develop the concept of size, to have an idea what say 5 marbles and 5 footballs look like.

ADDITION

At first this is adding one more. This should begin by adding an extra item to a pile and asking the child to find out how many there are now. Keep the numbers small and allow plenty of practice before transferring the 'game' to paper. Reinforcement consolidates providing it is not allowed to become boring. It is essential to work at the pace of the child. Too slowly and interest is lost, too quickly and confusion leads to fear. Children have short concentration spans but absorb information like sponges.

When the child is confident about counting to 10 and understands what he or she is doing then more addition can be done and in different ways.

SUBTRACTION

This usually begins with 'take away', how many are left? Take away strips are useful with the child crossing out the object to be taken away. Finding the difference between two quantities can be regarded as a form of matching. Adding on will be met in shopping. Shopping is a particularly good activity because children have experience of it. A classroom shop is a must and later, picture shopping allows more variety.

ESTIMATING

This is a particularly valuable skill used daily by us all. Children soon begin to recognise 'silly' answers. Begin with say 5 then 2 then 8 objects. The concepts of size, volume and quantity have to be developed. 100 marbles may go into a jar, 100 footballs will not. Estimating skills develop. How many marbles, how many tennis balls, how many footballs can be put in a desk or a box? What happens when the box chosen is smaller or bigger? It is important that children learn what numbers are sensible. This is an invaluable skill to develop. As adults we are bombarded with numbers and data that question our credulity.

ORDERING

As their concept of numbers develops, children need practice in placing them in their correct positions. When the physical idea of cardinal numbers has been grasped then pictures and drawings can be used. But do not move children too quickly to written arithmetic.

Ordinal numbers should follow. The idea that one block can be picked up and given the ordinal number, for

example, third is not a natural one. Children will be used to queuing and this is useful experience. They understand being first, second and last in a queue.

MONEY

Children meet money as pocket money and as presents. The classroom shop and car boot sale give them plenty of practice. Show the relationship between different coins and £1. Discuss the importance of tens.

    10   10 pence pieces make £1
    10   5 pence pieces make 50p
     5   10 pence pieces make 50p
    10   2 pence pieces make 20p
     2   10 pence pieces make 20p

HALVES AND QUARTERS

Children are used to having half or less of what adults eat. Initially, children can work with the idea of a half as one of two pieces not necessarily of the same size. They need practice in halving a variety of items such as a peeled orange, a piece of plasticine and a handful of beads or marbles. As the concept of equal parts develops, they have to think of ways in which to divide exactly into two - counting, weighing, folding and so on. The division of 50p into two introduces more suggestions. The work is then extended into quarters. Here they need to divide a half again using say an orange, Cuisenaire rods or Colour Factor. Their experience may include cooking - half a cup, half a block of butter, and sharing food in the family or with friends. They will also be familiar with some of the class taking part in different activities such as swimming. When they have a firm idea of what is meant by a half and a quarter it is safe to transfer to drawings on paper. Let children estimate half or quarter of the size of objects such as the length of a broom handle or the height of a door...

MEASURING AND UNITS

Children need practice in measuring and estimating.
Non-uniform non standard units. Let them decide how they can measure things in the classroom using handspans, strides, feet, crayons, pencils... They soon realise that these units are unsatisfactory. The question why do people get different answers starts a lively discussion often with surprising comments. They need to know the meaning of such words as half full, half empty.
Uniform non standard units. Multilink, Cuisenaire Rods, Unifix, playing cards and coins.
Standard Units. Although the basic standard is SI units, children are already used to a mixture of units - a quarter of sweets, a gallon of petrol and a litre of milk...

Practical work is essential if children are to gain an understanding of measuring and units that will benefit them all their lives.

Children need to accept the conservation of length, to accept that moving an object does not change its length. Suppose a desk measures 'seven pencils' across. At first the child needs to see seven pencils laid end to end. Only later will it be acceptable to use one pencil and place it repeatedly seven times across the desk. Children believe what they see. (A kind of wisdom lost when we grow up.) If two pencils are of the same length and one juts out, then they are likely to think that the one jutting out is longer than the other. At all times encourage the children to estimate size.

The stages are

  Direct comparison - he/she is shorter, taller than...
  Indirect comparison - with some agreed mark on a chart.
  Indirect comparison using several units laid end to end.
  Indirect comparison with one unit repeated many times.
  Measuring using uniform units.
  Measuring using standard units.
  Computations involving SI units.

Units are needed for length, area, capacity, weight (mass) and time.

NUMBERS IN WORDS AND FIGURES

It is important that children learn number facts and skills in context and that they practise them in a practical way so that the work is relevant to everyday life.

SUMS TO 10 AND 20
NUMBERS TO 1000

They must feel the work is creative, exciting and fun. Use games as much as possible. Children need to know the importance of place value.

MULTIPLICATION AND DIVISION

It is debatable whether to teach division before multiplication because children learn about 'sharing' at a very early stage.

Division is sharing or repeated subtraction. Children need practice in sharing things out equally (dealing cards, dividing piles of marbles and counters) and in moving backwards along a number line. Arrays and squares of counters are helpful.

Mulitplication is repeated addition and children begin with groups or sets. Small groups (say 2 or 5 marbles) are laid out in rows and counted so that the children understand the number in one row, two rows, three rows, and so on. That is two lots, three lots...

It is important that they understand that mulitplication involves numbers of identical sets and develop a sense of pattern.

NUMBER PATTERNS

Mark every 2nd figure in a 0 to 99 number square so that 2 and all multiples of 2 are coloured. [If this is too

tedious, use half the square or let some of the class do different sections of the square and then put them together.] This shows the pattern and gives a 'feel' as to how the numbers behave. Make a 0 - 99 number square on 2 cm squared paper and use with Multilink. Place say a red block on every even number, a green one on every 2nd number and a yellow on every 10th number. This builds up a 3D picture of factors and products. Children soon understand what is happening when more than one colour occurs on a square.

Examine the way in which a rectangle with 10 or 20 squares can be drawn.

Commutativity. It is important that children understand this. The equivalence of 5 x 2 and 2 x 5 can be shown by rearranging five groups of 2 marbles into two groups of 5 marbles. The children will suggest more examples. [This is also shown in a 1 - 10 multiplication square.

```
 1   2   3   4   5   6   7   8   9  10
 2   4   6   8  10  12  14  16  18  20
 3   6   9  12  15  18  21  24  27  30
 4   8  12  16  20  24  28  32  36  40
 5  10  15  20  25  30  35  40  45  50
 6  12  18  24  30  36  42  48  54  60
 7  14  21  28  35  42  49  56  63  70
 8  16  24  32  40  48  56  64  72  80
 9  18  27  36  45  54  63  72  81  90
10  20  30  40  50  60  70  80  90 100
```

Children need to make this square on large squared paper. It is symmetrical about its leading diagonal. This shows commutativity clearly, that is 2 x 5 is the same as 5 x 2 in the square and so on. When children are learning tables they need to learn only half of them.]

Consider 25 ÷ 5. Use 5 rows of 5 counters or Multilink, then 5 can be taken away five times. Repeat with several numbers and factors until the children are confident. Once they understand that division is the opposite process to multiplication they will obtain answers from their tables.

Long multiplication and long division are now almost always done with calculators.

RELATIONSHIPS BETWEEN DIFFERENT OPERATIONS

Children should be able to understand the relationship between the four operations and a simple diagram helps.

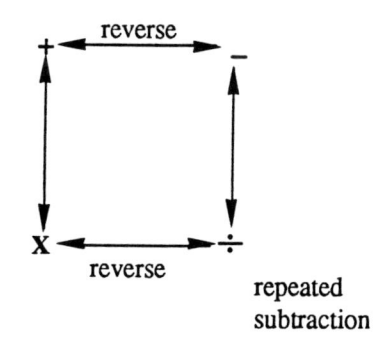

```
              reverse
        +  ←—————————→  -
        ↑               ↑
        ↓               ↓
        X  ←—————————→  ÷
              reverse
repeated                    repeated
addition                    subtraction
```

FUNCTION MACHINES

Function machines encourage children to find answers to Why? How? and What if? In/Out exercises with a secret constant or operation fed into the machine can only be done by trial and error and by discovering the relationship between the numbers fed into the machine and those coming out. LOGO is particularly useful at this stage. Function machines help children learn about repetitive operations and to handle different operations - finding the number that comes out and then the number that went in.

Look for patterns in addition and multiplication squares, and explore ways of tackling calculations.

TIME

Begin with the activities children know about: the structure of the day - the time they get up, have breakfast, go to school, when school starts and finishes, the time they go home. Go on to ways in which time can be measured. including a water clock, an egg timer, a candle clock, a sundial, shadow clock and pendulum clock. Discuss the clocks the children have at home leading to analogue and digital clocks and watches. Discuss how time 'feels' and why it seems to pass slowly or quickly.

Telling the Time. Begin with the hours and go on to half and quarter hours - quarter to and quarter past, big hands and small hands on clock faces. Explain minutes and seconds. Children find it easy to read digital clocks but are not always sure what they mean. Make a time chart for the day and individual timetables. Estimate how much can be done in three minutes, how long it takes to tidy the room, change for PE, travel home, length of a lesson. Children can close their eyes and raise their hands when they think a minute has passed.

Time on a Longer Scale. Other ways in which the passing of time is measured: days, weeks, months and years. Make a calendar and relate the months to seasons and annual events such as holidays and festivals. The importance of measuring time - schedules and timetables, time zones. Look at photographs and newspapers to illustrate changes with time and the idea of past, present and future. What will children be doing tomorrow, at the weekend, on their holidays? Children often confuse size with age - bigger seems to mean older. They understand candles on a birthday cake. Plan a journey. Look at timetables for buses and trains and possible routes for going by car. Make a time line starting 15 years ago to the end of the century.

ZERO AND NEGATIVE NUMBERS

Discuss the situations in which zero is used in everyday life. The weather forecast uses zero and there is a zero on a thermometer. Zero is essential as a 'place holder'. Children will also see it easily in the pattern of 10s.

Negative Numbers. These can be difficult to accept and it may be necessary to return to them again at a later stage. Initially, they may be considered as below zero. If zero is taken as the base mark then above this, numbers are positive and below they are zero. Two illustrations help. First, use a thermometer with 0° for freezing on the

Celsius scale. Negative temperatures represent those below freezing. Next, consider a lift. If the ground floor is zero, the floor above is floor 1 while the basement is -1. Negative numbers can be shown on a number line. In one way, negative numbers are a mathematical contrivance, a device enabling us to handle such situations as

$$2 - 5 = -3$$

Later, Children have to learn the rules that allow them to handle negative numbers.

SORTING

Being able to sort and classify are very important skills. They form the basis of organisation. Begin with things familiar to the children. They will have no difficulty in sorting a mixed pile of gloves, shoes, hats and scarves or sorting them out in a different way according to their owners. Each group forms a set. Children are familiar with laundry being sorted out at home - whites, coloureds, delicates, hot water wash. Choices are often intuitive but they should be able to explain their selections.

Attribute cards help to develop ways of choosing and organising. These can be drawn to vary in two or more ways. For example 25 to 30 cards can be drawn of a teapot which has or does not have a spout or a handle. This gives rise to several sets. [With handle and spout, without handle and spout, with handle but no spout and with spout but no handle. The teapots can be the same or different.] These notes contain a sheet of cards of black, white and ginger cats. [With whiskers and tails, with whiskers and no tail, with tail and no whiskers and without tail and whiskers).

Sets and Complements. Most early work concentrates on belonging or not belonging. This leads to dealing with objects that belong to more than one set. For example a collection of red plastic objects in one set and a collection of wooden blocks in another set. What happens to a red wooden block?

Intersection and Union. It can be difficult for children to accept that something can belong to two sets at the same time. Use large hoops on the floor so that there is good visual impact. Details of pets owned by the class lead to a set of dogs, a set of cats, a set of rabbits and so on. These, it is easily understood, all belong to a bigger set of pets. It is often not necessary or desirable to use the words 'intersection' and 'union'.

Venn Diagrams. The hoops lead on to Venn diagrams. Start with familiar situations - breakfast foods, the way in which children travel to school, favourite TV programmes or sports.

'WEIGHT'

What is meant by 'weight'. How are things weighed? Use a variety of scales including bathroom scales, kitchen scales, spring balance and classroom balance. Discuss units and the need for different kinds of scales and units. How would you weigh a button, a baby, an adult, an animal? What units would be used? Use marbles as weights before going on to standard weights. This is an area where children can have plenty of practice at estimating. First of all which is heavier or lighter and then estimates of actual weights. Children can also balance themselves on a seesaw and note what happens as they move further from or closer to the fulcrum. (No theory about this, of course.) Use non standard units and then standard units. (Pounds, half pounds, quarters, ounces, kilograms, grams.) How is food sold by weight in shops? Look at labels. Cooking gives excellent practice. Vary recipies according to the number of portions or cakes/biscuits/burgers needed. Weigh bread or cake over a period of a week and note what happens to the weight. Why does this happen?

CALCULATORS

As calculators come to be used more freely, it is possible to tackle different kinds of work. Calculators do not necessarily mean that children do not have to learn their tables or basic arithmetic. Estimated answers ensure that the principles and methods involved are understood. Suppose a child is asked to find two consecutive numbers which when mulitplied together equal 1260. This is tedious by traditional methods. [Estimation suggests the numbers lie between 30 and 40. The calculator gives 34 x 35 = 1190 and 35 x 36 = 1260.] The calculator offers a good way of testing if place value is understood. The child is asked to remove the digits of a 3 or 4 digit number one at a time by subtraction until zero is left. To eliminate say 853 it is necessary to subtract 3, 50 and 800 (in any order). Clear thinking is encouraged by using calculators as function machines. A constant operation (say 5 x) is fed into the calculator and the children then feed in a series of numbers pressing the = button after each number is fed in. The numbers in and the numbers out are recorded on paper and the process repeated without touching the clear button. From a series of readings, the children work out the value of the constant.

INVESTIGATIONS AND PROBLEM SOLVING

Investigation. This is fundamental to all subjects but it is particularly important in mathematics. It is vital in the process of developing mathematical thinking.

Children acquire information which has to be sorted and classified. They then hypothesize, test and predict. A high degree of organisation is needed. The question 'What if . . .?' calls for logical and hypothetical proposals.They have to be prepared to revise ideas and evaluate negative evidence. Finally, they have to justify and explain their discoveries and conclusions to others.

Problem Solving. When problems are tackled in groups, children learn social skills as well. They learn to co-operate, to listen to each other, discuss other people's ideas, to try out suggestions and to allow others and themselves to be wrong.

DATA

We are surrounded by an ever increasing avalanche of information and technical data. Learning to extract infor-

mation that is relevant and useful to us is a valuable skill. Learning how to represent information in a way that makes it easy to understand is also important. A study of advertising gives endless examples of the ways in which information is analysed and presented. Children's comments on such material usually show remarkable discernment.

Begin with the familiar such as a pile of mixed clothing. Children need to understand that with a universal set of data there may be subsets defined by different characteristics or attributes. It is necessary to decide how the data is to be sorted. This depends on the kind of data and the nature of the investigation, that is the kind of conclusions to be drawn. For example, consider a pile of mixed clothing - scarves, gloves, mittens, socks, shoes, hats . . . Is the investigation about the number of scarves, the number of gloves (in pairs or singles?) or is it about who wears what, or is it about the colour or kind of material used to make the clothes? Is it about whether they can go in the washing machine together? The information to be collected will decide how the items are to be sorted, what sets are to be created : a set of scarves, a set of gloves . . . or a set of John's clothing, a set of Mary's clothing . . .

Mostly, the data cannot be physically sorted in this way but is recorded as information on paper. The way in which it is to be recorded is very important.

Information The children should discuss what information is needed.
Information Record Sheet They should plan how the information is to be recorded. Allow for the unexpected.
Observations Decide how the information is to be obtained - by observation or questionnaire . . . If we do not make the relevant observations or ask the appropriate questions then we shall not collect the data we need. Discuss whether the way in which observations are made or questions worded will affect the replies. It is surprisingly difficult to ask the 'right questions'. Often national surveys costing large amounts of money are flawed because the questions are poorly worded.
Conclusions Decide the nature of the results.
Using the results The conclusions may not be what is expected. Discuss the ways in which the results can be presented and the effects of these different presentations.

LISTS AND TABLES

These are probably the simplest way of handling data. They may be organised in several ways such as alphabetically, by size, by geographical location, in order of importance and so on. Children will be familiar with shopping lists, party lists - guests and games, lists of tasks at home and so on.
Tally and Frequency Tables These are particularly useful when counting is involved as in, for example, an analysis of traffic. The children simply mark on their record sheet each time they count one of the vehicles. One child or a pair counts one kind of vehicle only and the class results are put together.

GRAPHS AND DATA

Picture Graphs In these information is represented by drawings or pictures. Later one picture can represent a number or group of items. For example, initially one car may represent one vehicle, later children can learn to let it represent say 10 cars and so handle bigger numbers.
Block Graphs In these each column is discrete and the blocks are clearly marked. Each column has its own label.
Bar Graphs The blocks used in block graphs are replaced by continuous bars.

VENN DIAGRAMS
CARROLL DIAGRAMS

These are useful for displaying the relationships between sets of objects. They are easy to understand and present a simple way of dealing with items with attributes that place them in two or more sets.

CO-ORDINATES

Two skills are developed when plotting points. There is the ability to read across and down as when reading a timetable and the understanding that the position of a point can be determined by an ordered pair of numbers or a number and a letter. Begin with 'finding objects on simple squared paper such as on a treasure map.

A map of the school and its surroundings extends the work into a practical application and can be followed by a map of where a child lives. Much can be learned from making a detailed street map in which the squares rather than the lines are numbered. The work is difficult involving children pacing the streets and using compasses.

SHAPE AND SPACE
LEVELS 1 - 3

2-D SHAPES

Children should have had experience in sorting shapes of all types and should be able to recognise 2-D shapes. They need to recognise squares, rectangles, circles, triangles, hexagons and pentagons and be able to describe their properties.

Squares and Rectangles. They should know in which ways these are similar and in which ways they are different. Squares are special kinds of rectangles. Distinguish between circles and ovals.

ANGLES

Children should first see an angle as a measurement of the 'amount of turn or rotation'. An angle should be seen as dynamic not static. There are numerous examples from door handles to cooker knobs, from wheels to water taps. Estimating angles is a worthwhile skill to develop.

Right Angles. These are everywhere: the angle at the elbow can be a right angle as can the angle between the thumb and the hand. Look for right angles in the classroom, then identify them in squares, rectangles and right-angled triangles.

Compass. Relate angles to the points of the compass. Find north. In which direction is the school hall, the playground? Look at maps and discuss the ways in which a compass helps travellers. Discuss how to use a map of your town or area.

3-D SHAPES

The world is a 3-D place. Look at 3-D shapes in the classroom and discuss common factors. Then study a selection of 3-D mathematical shapes.

Cube. Six faces, each face being a square. Look for the right-angles. Three faces meet at each corner or vertex.

Cubes and Cuboids. Discuss where these can be found. Cubes - ice cube, sugar, stock, die.

Cuboids - suitcase, computer, shoe box, pencil box. Count faces and corners. Cut open a box and discuss the changes this makes.

Cylinders. Let children collect examples. Cut open the cardboard roll of a toilet roll and examine the change this makes to the shape. Let children make a cylinder.

Cylinders - vacuum cleaner, hose pipe, pencil, washing-up liquid container.

Spheres. Collect spheres of different sizes - marbles, beads, tennis balls.

WORDS OF POSITION

Children need to relate the position of one object to another.

MOVEMENT

In PE have children move in one direction (translational) and then turn (rotational) or flip over. In Art, children can paint with blocks and move the blocks sideways or turn them.

They should understand turning clockwise or anti-clockwise.

SYMMETRY

The idea of symmetry is based on the premise that things can be moved around and still look the same. Children often have an instinctive understanding of symmetry and will make their drawings and models as symmetrical as they can. Children can make drawings with matching halves and 'butterfly' ink blots in the fold of a piece of paper. Use safe plastic mirrors and drawings and pictures to make examples of symmetry. Make half drawings that will be complete when viewed in the mirror. Place a mirror on letters and drawings and examine the reflections. Discuss the symmetry of letters, numbers and 2-D shapes.

Hundred Square

1	2	3	4	5	6	7	8	9	10
11	12	13	14	15	16	17	18	19	20
21	22	23	24	25	26	27	28	29	30
31	32	33	34	35	36	37	38	39	40
41	42	43	44	45	46	47	48	49	50
51	52	53	54	55	56	57	58	59	60
61	62	63	64	65	66	67	68	69	70
71	72	73	74	75	76	77	78	79	80
81	82	83	84	85	86	87	88	89	90
91	92	93	94	95	96	97	98	99	100

ATTRIBUTE CARDS

Maths KS1 Master File © E J P & D C P

Teachers' Notes/Attribute Cards 98

TWO-CENTIMETRE SQUARED PAPER

CENTIMETRE SQUARED PAPER

DOTTY PAPER (SQUARES)

DOTTY PAPER (TRIANGLES)

RECORD SHEET
MATHEMATICS

Name _____   Age _____

Page	Master Copy		Page	Master Copy	
4	Colour to Sort		47	Odd and Even Numbers	
5	Sorting as Sets		48	An Add 3 Robot	
6	Sorting by Type		49	A Take Away 4 Robot	
7	Match and Colour		50	Multiplication/Counting On	
8	Matching Shapes		51	2, 5, and 10 (Hundred Square)	
9	How Many?		52	Multiply Squares	
10	Counting Objects		53	Bingo (Multiplication)	
11	Writing/Counting Numbers (1, 2)		54	Tens and Units	
12	Writing/Counting Numbers (3, 4)		55	Matching Numbers	
13	Writing/Counting Numbers (5, 6, 7)		56	Bingo (Addition)	
14	Counting		57	Sums to 20	
15	Writing/Counting Numbers (8, 9)		58	Sums to 20	
16	Counting to 10		59	Numbers to 1000	
17	Add 1		60	Numbers to 1000	
18	1 to 10		61	Numbers in Words	
19	Snow White (1 - 10)		62	Division	
20	Flowers (3, 4, 5)		63	Multiplication	
21	Conservation of Numbers		64	Units	
22	Addition		65	Measuring	
23	Add		66	Money	
24	Make 5		67	Time	
25	Make 10		68	More Time	
26	How Many Leaves?		69	Negative Numbers	
27	Take Away Strips		70	Lists	
28	Subtraction		71	Linking	
29	Add or Subtract		72	Count and Record	
30	Add (Vertical Addition)		73	Picture Graphs	
31	Take Away (Vertical Subtraction)		74	Picture Graphs	
32	Find the Missing Numbers		75	Waiting for the Bus	
33	Estimates		76	Bar Graphs	
34	Left Luggage		77	Weather Chart	
35	Ordering		78	Sorting and Recording	
36	Catch a Falling Star		79	Position	
37	Money		80	Measuring Words	
38	Shopping		81	2-D Shapes	
39	Car Boot Sale		82	3-D Shapes	
40	Half		83	Matching Shapes and Sides	
41	Quarter		84	Angles	
42	Measuring using Non-Standard Units		85	Moving	
43	Measuring and Comparing		86	Symmetry	
44	Measures - Standard Units		87	Co-ordinates	
45	Patterns - Shapes and Colours		88	Points of the Compass	
46	Number Bonds		89	Clockwise or Anti-clockwise?	

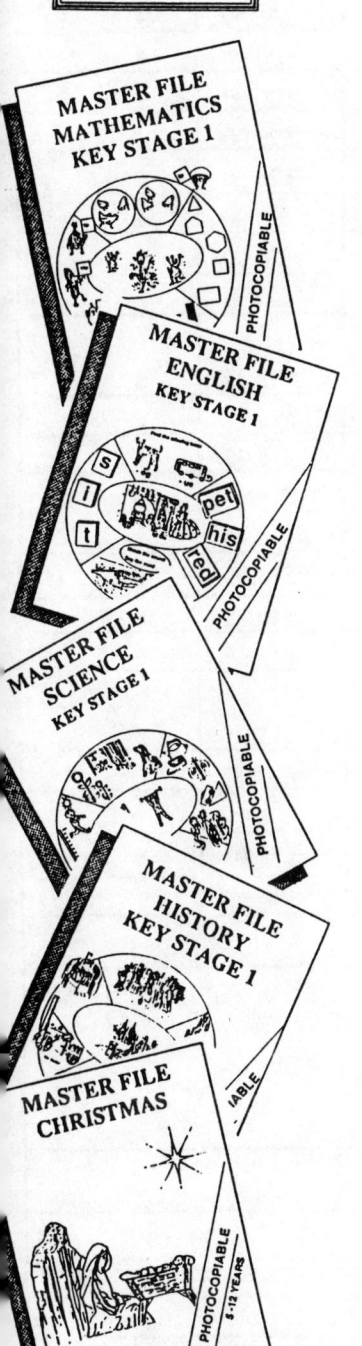

MASTER FILES

published by
Domino Books (Wales) Ltd.

AN ESTABLISHED SERIES
prepared by experienced teachers

- NOTES FOR TEACHERS AND WORKSHEETS FOR PUPILS IN ONE BOOK
- COMPREHENSIVE NATIONAL CURRICULUM COVERAGE
- THERE IS NO NEED TO BUY ADDITIONAL MATERIAL
- ALL THE MATERIAL IS PHOTOCOPIABLE
- EXCELLENT VALUE
- SAVES YOU TIME AND MONEY
- VISUALLY STIMULATING
- BOOKS SPECIFICALLY DESIGNED FOR THE KEY STAGE YOU TEACH
- FULL OF TEACHING STRATEGIES AND IDEAS
- READY-TO-USE LESSONS
- FLEXIBLE RESOURCES FOR USE BY THE WHOLE CLASS, BY GROUPS OR BY INDIVIDUAL PUPILS
- TRIED AND TESTED MATERIALS
- PHOTOCOPIABLE SHEETS TO USE AS THEY ARE OR TO REDUCE OR ENLARGE
- PHOTOCOPIABLE RECORD SHEETS FOR EACH PUPIL
- NEW TITLES PUBLISHED MONTHLY

AVAILABLE FROM
Domino Books (Wales) Ltd.,
P O Box 32, Swansea SA1 1FN.
Tel. (01792) 459378   Fax. (01792) 466337
Telephone and fax orders welcome

ORDER FORM OVERLEAF

MASTER FILES
ORDER FORM

KEY STAGE 1 (Age 5 - 7)   **KEY STAGE 2 (Age 7 - 11)**   **KEY STAGE 3 (Age 11 - 14)**

Quantity	Title	ISBN	Price	Cost
	MATHEMATICS (KS1)	1 85772 107 1	£20.00	£
	HISTORY (KS1)	1 85772 112 8	£20.00	£
	ENGLISH (KS1)	1 85772 111 X	£20.00	£
	SCIENCE (KS1)	1 85772 108 X	£20.00	£
	MATHEMATICS (KS2)	1 85772 086 5	£20.00	£
	ENGLISH (KS2)	1 85772 085 7	£20.00	£
	SCIENCE (KS2)	1 85772 087 3	£20.00	£
	MATHEMATICS (KS3)	1 85772 126 8	£20.00	£
	ENGLISH (KS3)	1 85772 127 6	£20.00	£
	SCIENCE (KS3)	1 85772 128 4	£20.00	£
	HISTORY			
	Invaders and Settlers - The Celts (KS2)	1 85772 067 9	£15.95	£
	Invaders and Settlers - The Romans (KS2)	1 85772 070 9	£15.95	£
	Invaders and Settlers - Anglo-Saxons (KS2)	1 85772 068 7	£15.95	£
	Invaders and Settlers - The Vikings (KS2)	1 85772 069 5	£15.95	£
	Life in Tudor Times (KS2)	1 85772 076 8	£15.95	£
	Victorian Britain (KS2 - KS3)	1 85772 077 6	£15.95	£
	The Second World War (KS2 - KS3)	1 85772 121 7	£15.95	£
	The Twentieth Century World (KS2 - KS3)	1 85772 074 1	£15.95	£
	TOPICS			
	Castles (KS2 - KS3)	1 85772 075 X	£15.95	£
	Christmas (Ages 5 - 12)	1 85772 065 2	£20.00	£
	NEW FOR NURSERY CLASSES			
	First Steps (Basic Activities in the 3Rs)	1 85772 130 6	£12.50	£
		Total	£	

Name/Organisation/School

Address

Post Code   Tel.

Contact   Signature

Order Number   Date

Available from Foyles Bookshop, Welsh Books Council, Blackwells, Georges, Bookland, Dillons, Hammicks, Waterstones, WH Smith and all good booksellers or direct from
DOMINO BOOKS (WALES) LTD, P O BOX 32, SWANSEA SA1 1FN
TEL. 01792 459378   FAX. 01792 466337

All official orders must have an official requisition form attached (schools, educational establishments, LEAs, bookshops, libraries). Cheques with private orders please.